ELINES OF HISTORY
VOLUME 3

RAIDERS AND CONQUERORS

500–1000 A.D.

GROLIER

an imprint of

SCHOLASTIC

www.scholastic.com/librarypublishing

Published by Grolier,
an imprint of Scholastic Library Publishing,
Sherman Turnpike
Danbury, Connecticut 06816

© 2005 The Brown Reference Group plc

Set ISBN 0-7172-6002-X
Volume 3 ISBN 0-7172-6005-4

Library of Congress Cataloging-in-Publication Data

Timelines of history.
        p. cm.
    Includes index.
    Contents: v. 1. The early empires, prehistory—500 B.C. —
v. 2. The classical age, 500 B.C.—500 A.D. — v. 3. Raiders and
conquerors, 500—1000 — v. 4. The feudal era, 1000—1250 —
v. 5. The end of the Middle Ages, 1250—1500 — v. 6. A wider
world, 1500—1600 — v. 7. Royalty and revolt, 1600—1700 —
v. 8. The Age of Reason, 1700—1800 — v. 9. Industry and
empire, 1800—1900 — v. 10. The modern world, 1900—2000.
    ISBN 0-7172-6002-X (set : alk. paper) — ISBN 0-7172-
6003-8 (v. 1 : alk. paper) — ISBN 0-7172-6004-6 (v. 2 : alk.
paper) — ISBN 0-7172-6005-4 (v. 3 : alk. paper) — ISBN 0-
7172-6006-2 (v. 4 : alk. paper) — ISBN 0-7172-6007-0 (v. 5 :
alk. paper) — ISBN 0-7172-6008-9 (v. 6 : alk. paper) — ISBN
0-7172-6009-7 (v. 7 : alk. paper) — ISBN 0-7172-6010-0 (v. 8
: alk.paper) — ISBN 0-7172-6011-9 (v. 9 : alk. paper) —
ISBN 0-7172-6012-7 (v. 10 : alk. paper)
    1. Chronology, Historical

For information address the publisher:
Grolier, Sherman Turnpike,
Danbury, Connecticut 06816

Printed and bound in Thailand

FOR THE BROWN REFERENCE GROUP PLC

Consultant: Professor Jeremy Black, University of Exeter

Project Editor: Tony Allan
Designers: Frankie Wood
Picture Researcher: Sharon Southren
Cartographic Editor: Tim Williams
Design Manager: Lynne Ross
Production: Alastair Gourlay, Maggie Copeland
Senior Managing Editor: Tim Cooke
Editorial Director: Lindsey Lowe
Writers: Windsor Chorlton, Penny Isaacs, Susan Kennedy,
Michael Kerrigan

PICTURE CREDITS
(t = top, b = bottom, c = center, l = left, r = right)

Cover
Corbis: Christie's Images b.

AKG-images: British Library 6b, Erich Lessing 46r; ©**Philip
Baird/www.anthroarcheart.org:** 29, 41t; **Corbis:** 24b, Archivo
Iconografico, S.A. 6t, 8t, 10l, 11, 12t, 19b, 26l, 40l, 45b, Austrian
Archives 44, Bettmann 18t, 40b, Christie's Images 23, James
Davis/Eye Ubiquitous 45t, Macduff Everton 20t, Randy Faris 15,
Lowell Georgia 9, Chris Hellier 28t, Charles & Josette Lenars 33l,
Frances G.Mayer 33r, Kevin R.Morris 36b, Richard T.Nowitz 24t,
Royal Ontario Museum 13b, Kevin Schafer 25t, Seattle Museum
27t, Stapleton Collection 37l, Sygma/Maher Attar 22r, Rugero
Vanni 31, Brian Vikander 16b, Adam Woolfitt 37r, Jane
Wishnetsky 12b, Roger Wood 22l, 25b, Michael S.Yamashita 27b;
DigitalVision: Jeremy Woodhouse 36t, 42r; **Hamill Gallery of
African Art, Boston, MA:** 41l; **Robert Harding Picture Library:**
Robert Frerck 14t; Peter Langer, Associated Media Group: 17;
Network Photographers: Georg Gerster 26b; **Otago Museum,
Dunedin, New Zealand:** 32; **PA Photos:** EPA 43; **Photos.com:**
21; **Rex Features Ltd:** Pacific Press Service 18b; **South American
Pictures:** Tony Morrison 34b; **TopFoto.co.uk:** HIP 18b; The
Image Works/David Frazier 28b; **Werner Forman Archive:** 42l,
45cl, Museum fur Volkerkunde, Berlin 13t.

CONTENTS

HOW TO USE THIS BOOK

INTRODUCTION

The 500-year period covered in this volume was one of new beginnings, conquest, and consolidation. After 500 A.D. western Europe entered the "Dark Ages" as Germanic warlords created new kingdoms in the ruins of the Roman Empire; amid the chaos only the Christian church kept alive Rome's legacy of law and learning. By the end of the 10th century most of Europe except the far north had become Christian. In the 8th century A.D. Charlemagne, the greatest ruler of early medieval Europe, united France, Italy, and much of Germany, but his empire broke up after his death, when Christian Europe came under attack from Viking raiders from Scandinavia.

One of the most important events for history was the birth of a new religion, Islam, founded by the Prophet Muhammad in the 7th century A.D. Arab armies sweeping out of the Arabian deserts spread Islam through West Asia into North Africa and Spain, along the coast of East Africa, and across Central Asia. They built a civilization that in terms of art, literature, science, and scholarship far outshone that of Europe, although the unity of the Arab world was weakened by the division of Islam into Shiite and Sunni branches and the overthrow of the Umayyad Dynasty of caliphs by the Abbasids in 750 A.D.

China enjoyed a period of stability under the Tang Dynasty (618–907 A.D.), and Japan was brought under the rule of the Yamato emperors. Mexico was dominated by the city of Teotihuacan until its destruction about 700 A.D., while the Maya cities of the Guatemalan lowlands were in decline. The early Pueblo farmers of the American Southwest built complex cliff cities, and in Oceania Polynesian voyagers were spreading through the scattered island groups of the South Pacific.

ABBREVIATIONS	
mi	miles
cm	centimeters
m	meters
km	kilometers
sq. km	square kilometers
mya	million years ago
c.	about (from the Latin word circa)

A NOTE ON DATES

This set follows standard Western practice in dating events from the start of the Christian era, presumed to have begun in the year 0. Those that happened before the year 0 are listed as B.C. (before the Christian era), and those that happened after as A.D. (from the Latin Anno Domini, meaning "in the year of the Lord"). Wherever possible, exact dates are given; where there is uncertainty, the date is prefixed by the abbreviation c. (short for Latin circa, meaning "about") to show that it is approximate.

ABOUT THIS SET

This book is one of a set of ten providing timelines for world history from the beginning of recorded history up to 2000 A.D. Each volume arranges events that happened around the world within a particular period and is made up of three different types of facing two-page spreads: timelines, features, and glossary pages ("Facts at a Glance," at the back of the book). The three should be used in combination to find the information that you need. Timelines list events that occurred between the dates shown on the pages and cover periods ranging from several centuries at the start of Volume 1, dealing with early times, to six or seven years in Volumes 9 and 10, addressing the modern era.

In part, the difference reflects the fact that much more is known about recent times than about distant eras. Yet it also reflects a real acceleration in the number of noteworthy events, related to surging population growth. Demographers estimate that it was only in the early 19th century that world population reached one billion; at the start of the 21st century the figure is over six billion and rising, meaning that more people have lived in the past 200 years than in all the other epochs of history combined.

The subjects covered by the feature pages may be a major individual or a civilization. Some cover epoch-making events, while others address more general themes such as the development of types of technology. In each case the feature provides a clear overview of its subject to supplement its timeline entries, indicating its significance on the broader canvas of world history.

Facts at a Glance lists names and terms that may be unfamiliar or that deserve more explanation than can be provided in the timeline entries. Check these pages for quick reference on individuals, peoples, battles, or cultures, and also for explanations of words that are not clear.

The comprehensive index at the back of each book covers the entire set and will enable you to follow all references to a given subject across the ten volumes.

TIMELINE PAGES

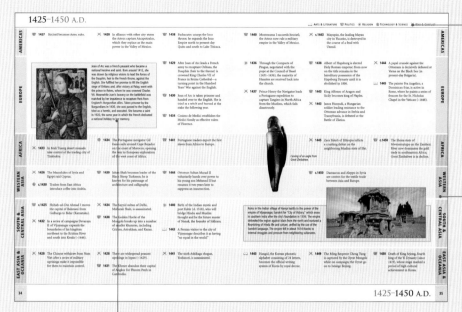

Symbols
Each entry is prefixed by one of five symbols—for example, crossed swords for war, an open book for arts and literature—indicating a particular category of history. A key to the symbols is printed at the top of the right-hand page.

Bands
Each timeline is divided into five or six bands relating to different continents or other major regions of the world. Within each band events are listed in chronological (time) order.

Boxes
Boxes in each timeline present more detailed information about important individuals, places, events, or works.

FEATURE PAGES

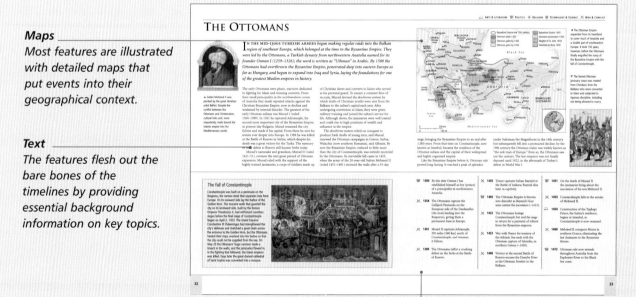

Maps
Most features are illustrated with detailed maps that put events into their geographical context.

Text
The features flesh out the bare bones of the timelines by providing essential background information on key topics.

Subject-specific timelines
Each feature has a timeline devoted exclusively to its topic to give an at-a-glance overview of the main developments in its history.

THE BYZANTINE EMPIRE

▲ The Emperor Justinian holds a golden bowl in this mosaic from the Church of San Vitale in Ravenna, Italy. Justinian presided over the Byzantine Empire at the time of its greatest expansion. He also codified Roman law and rebuilt Constantinople's great cathedral, St. Sophia.

T HE BYZANTINE EMPIRE DEVELOPED *out of the eastern half of the Roman Empire. In the process it became something quite distinct. Although its rulers called themselves "kings of the Romans," oriental influences gradually eroded Roman traditions. Greek ousted Latin as the official language, and Orthodox Christianity replaced Roman Catholicism as the state religion. The emperors also introduced a type of feudal system, granting lands to warriors in return for military service; in so doing, they created a landowning aristocracy (upper class) that came to challenge their own power.*

Byzantium's first great emperor was also the last truly Roman ruler. Justinian I, who came to the throne in 527, spoke Latin, assembled the heritage of Roman law into one body, and attempted to restore imperial rule in the west. Belisarius, his leading general, recovered North Africa from the Vandals and then embarked on a 20-year struggle to drive the Ostrogoths from Italy.

Justinian's gains were short-lived. Soon after his death the Lombards—another "barbarian" people—conquered northern Italy, while Avars, Bulgars, and Slavs depopulated much of the Balkans. Persian armies reached the walls of Constantinople in 609 and again in 625. Locked in a struggle for survival, the empire grew less and less concerned with the west. Greek replaced Latin as the official language of a Chinese-style bureaucracy famed for its secretiveness.

In 627 the Emperor Heraclius inflicted a crushing defeat on the Persians, only to be confronted shortly after by an even more formidable enemy. Arabs inspired by the new religion of Islam seized Palestine, Syria, and Egypt from Byzantine hands. They might have taken Constantinople itself but for the supremacy of the Byzantine navy and its secret weapon, "Greek fire"—an inflammable substance that was pumped over enemy ships.

Wars with the Arabs were partly responsible for a serious rift between the Orthodox ("right-believing") and Roman Catholic churches. In 726 the Emperor Leo III, who attributed the military successes of the Muslims to their strict ban on religious images, ordered the destruction of Byzantine icons—religious pictures and statues. When the news reached the pope in Rome, he denounced the emperor as a heretic. The Iconoclastic ("image-breaking") Controversy raged in Byzantium itself until icons were restored in 843. But by then the gulf between Byzantium and Rome was too wide to be bridged.

---

529 Justinian I codifies Roman law. In the same year he closes the Athens Academy founded by Plato.

534 In the opening move of a campaign to regain the Western Empire Justinian's leading general, Belisarius, takes North Africa from the Vandals.

542 Bubonic plague kills up to half the population of Constantinople (–543).

568 Lombards invade Italy and occupy most of the country north of the Po River.

572 Renewed warfare breaks out between Byzantium and Persia (–591).

Constantinople

Constantinople's position at the confluence of major sea and land trading routes helped make it the largest and most splendid city in Christian Europe. Built on a bluff controlling the seaway between the Black Sea and the Aegean, it included a deepwater harbor in an inlet called the Golden Horn. On the landward side a massive wall built in the 5th century resisted all enemies until 1204. The social hub of the city was the Hippodrome, where the public gathered to watch horse and chariot racing and theatrical performances. Below the Hippodrome palace buildings and classical monuments jostled with magnificent churches, including the 6th-century Hagia (Saint) Sophia (*right*), which remained the largest church in the world until 1547, when Michelangelo raised the dome of St. Peter's in Rome.

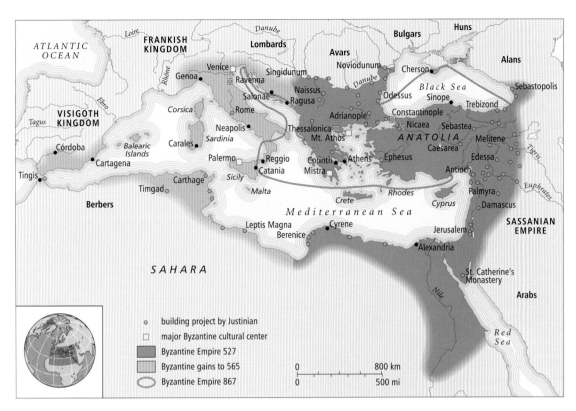

◀ The Byzantine Empire started out as the eastern half of the Roman Empire, which survived the fall of the Western Empire in the 5th century. Under Emperor Justinian and his brilliant general Belisarius the Byzantines managed to temporarily reconquer many of the lost western lands in the course of the 6th century. But the gains were short-lived. Under pressure from the Arabs the empire retrenched, and by the 9th century it was mostly restricted to the area of modern Turkey, Bulgaria, Greece, and the eastern Adriatic seaboard.

In response to the Arab threat the Byzantine rulers organized their territories into military districts called themes, governed by professional soldiers. The new system worked well, and Byzantium enjoyed a golden age under the Macedonian Dynasty founded by Basil I in 867. But the creation of military provinces also laid the foundation for the emergence of great landed families. These newly empowered nobles would jockey for imperial power during the 11th century, at a time when Byzantium faced new threats from Normans in the west and Turks in the east. Even so, the empire survived, although in a shrunken form, until 1453, when its capital Constantinople finally fell to the Ottoman Turks.

✕ **626** Emperor Heraclius survives a siege of Constantinople by an alliance of Persians, Slavs, and Avars, then (in 627) defeats the Persians decisively at Nineveh, in present-day Iraq.

✕ **637** Byzantium is seriously weakened by the Arab conquest of Mesopotamia, Syria, and (in 639) Egypt.

✕ **649** Arab pirates from Spain seize Cyprus from the Byzantines.

🏛 **663** Constans II makes the last visit to Rome by a Byzantine emperor.

✕ **673** An Arab fleet blockades Constantinople (–678).

✕ **717** Leo III repulses an Arab army besieging Constantinople and destroys its fleet (–718).

☀ **726** Leo III issues the first decrees banning the worship of icons and other religious images. His iconoclast policies open a rift with Rome and spark a bitter controversy at home that lasts until 843, when holy images are finally restored.

✕ **860** From their base in Russia Swedish Vikings known as Varangians mount their first attack on Constantinople.

🏛 **867** Basil I, an ex-horsebreaker who murdered his way to the Byzantine throne, establishes the Macedonian Dynasty.

✕ **880** Basil I reconquers Calabria (in southern Italy) from the Arabs.

📖 **945** After ruling for 30 years in the shadow of his father-in-law, Constantine VII seizes sole power. A guiding spirit of the Byzantine cultural revival, he encourages the compilation of historical writings.

✕ **961** Byzantines recapture Crete from the Arabs.

🏛 **976** Basil II, known as Bulgaroktonos ("Slayer of the Bulgars"), becomes Byzantine emperor.

🏛 **988** Basil II cements an alliance with Vladimir, prince of Kiev, who marries Basil's sister and converts to Orthodox Christianity.

🏛 **1453** The Byzantine Empire comes to an end when Constantinople falls to the Ottoman Turks.

AMERICAS

✳ **c.500** By this date North American hunters on the Great Plains are using the bow and arrow.

✳ **c.500** Ceramics in vivid colors are produced in many parts of Costa Rica and Panama.

👑 **c.500** Growing rich on the breeding of llamas and alpacas, the city of Tiahuanaco, to the south of Lake Titicaca in the Bolivian Andes, has by now spread its influence widely across the central Andes.

EUROPE

St. Benedict, shown in this 13th-century painting with his disciple St. Maur, has been called the father of Christian monasticism. His Rule, dividing the day into separate periods for work, study, and prayer, was hugely influential not just for his own Benedictine Order but also for all subsequent orders of monks. The son of a nobleman, Benedict put his precepts into practice at the monastery he founded at Monte Cassino, Italy.

⚔ **507** Alaric II, king of the Visigoths in Gaul, is killed in battle near Poitiers by the Frankish King Clovis.

👑 **511** Clovis, king of the Franks since 481, dies, and his realm is divided among his four sons, with courts at Paris, Metz, Soissons, and Orléans.

☀ **515** St. Benedict (c.480–547), the Italian founder of Western monasticism, composes his *Regula Monachorum* ("Monks' Rule"), which becomes the rule for monastic life in the west.

AFRICA

✳ **c.500** In South Africa's Transvaal seven fired earthenware heads are carefully buried—the most impressive works of Iron Age art yet discovered in southern Africa.

⚔ **c.523** Caleb, ruler of the Kingdom of Axum (Ethiopia), conquers the Yemen.

✳ **c.525** Cosmas Indicopleustes (meaning "Indian traveler"), a merchant of Alexandria, travels up the Nile to Ethiopia.

WESTERN ASIA

☀ **c.500** The Nestorians, a Christian sect that separated from the Orthodox Church in 431, settle in eastern Mesopotamia (Iraq).

⚔ **502** War breaks out between the Sassanian rulers of Persia and the Byzantine Empire. Neither side gains a clear advantage (–505).

⚔ **524** The Sassanians renew the war against the Byzantines, again with indecisive results (–531).

SOUTH & CENTRAL ASIA

⚔ **c.500** Toromana, a Hun leader, seizes the Punjab from India's Guptas.

👑 **c.500** The Buddhist trading state of Srivijaya emerges in Sumatra, modern Indonesia.

☀ **510** Suttee, a Hindu rite in which a widow dies on her husband's funeral pyre, is first recorded.

Carved wooden figures of musicians dating from the Gupta period in India.

EAST ASIA & OCEANIA

👑 **502** Xiao Yan founds China's Liang Dynasty after forcing Qi rulers to submit to his authority.

☀ **517** The Emperor Wu Ti becomes a Buddhist and introduces the new religion to central China.

☀ **523** The oldest known pagoda is built in China. Constructed in brick, it is a towerlike structure derived from the Buddhist stupa of India.

☀ **528** The Korean state of Silla adopts Buddhism; it is the last of the three kingdoms into which the Korean peninsula is divided to do so.

AMERICAS

👑 **c.504** Waterlily Jaguar, ruler of the southeastern Maya city of Copán, begins a major expansion of the city's ceremonial center, the Acropolis..

👑 **534** A mysterious lull sets in at Tikal, one of the main lowland Maya centers in Guatemala. Until 593 few monuments are erected.

👑 **537** A dated Maya inscription records that Double Bird is the 21st ruler of Tikal.

EUROPE

📖 **523** The Roman philosopher Boethius (c.480–524) writes his *De Consolatione Philosophiae* (The Consolations of Philosophy), which for the next millennium is one of the most widely read books after the Bible.

✴ **529** St. Benedict founds the monastery of Monte Cassino near Naples in Italy and establishes the Benedictine monastic order.

👑 **529** Justinian I (c.482–565), emperor of the Eastern Roman Empire, publishes his *Code of Civil Laws*, a work that will influence the law of most European countries down to modern times.

✕ **535** The Byzantine general Belisarius invades Italy.

✕ **c.537** Arthur, semilegendary king of the Britons, is killed in battle fighting Saxon invaders of Britain.

✴ **538** The church of St. Sophia in Constantinople, the first building with a large domed roof, is consecrated. It will remain the largest church in the Christian world until the 16th century.

⊕ **542** Bubonic plague, imported from Constantinople, ravages Europe for two years. Three further epidemics follow before the century's end.

✴ **c.550** St. David starts the conversion of Wales to Christianity.

AFRICA

✕ **534** The Byzantine general Belisarius overthrows the Vandal kingdom in North Africa and makes it a Byzantine province.

✴ **536** Justinian orders the closure of the temple of Philae on the Nile River, marking the official end of the cult of the ancient Egyptian gods.

WESTERN ASIA

👑 **531** Khusrow I (died 579) becomes ruler of the Sassanian Empire. Under his rule the empire reaches its greatest height.

👑 **533** Khusrow concludes the Endless Peace with the Byzantines. In fact, war breaks out again between the two powers just seven years later.

✕ **540** Khusrow's Sassanian army sacks the Byzantine city of Antioch on the Syrian coast.

SOUTH & CENTRAL ASIA

⊕ **c.520** Aryabhata, Hindu astronomer and mathematician (476–c.550), compiles a manual of astronomy. Aryabhata correctly states that the Earth rotates on its axis.

✕ **c.530** Yasodharman, a legendary hero from central India, is credited with repelling the invading Huns.

⊕ **c.550** The game of chess originates in the Indus Valley in India.

EAST ASIA & OCEANIA

⊕ **534** The Koreans introduce Chinese mathematics into Japan.

✕ **547** The Chinese crush a Vietnamese revolt led by Li-bon.

The tapering, multistoried buildings known as pagodas, usually associated with a temple complex, became East Asia's most distinctive form of religious architecture. Their shape derived from India's stupas—dome-shaped sanctuaries built to house Buddhist relics. The brick-built Pagoda of Songshan (*right*) is the oldest in China; it stands over 130 feet (40 m) high.

500–550 A.D.

9

THE FRANKISH KINGDOM

AS THE WESTERN ROMAN EMPIRE COLLAPSED, *barbarian warlords fought each other for land and power in the territories it had once ruled. The most enduringly successful was Clovis, king of the Franks from 481 to 511, who created a realm that extended from modern Belgium to the Mediterranean Sea. By the mid-6th century his successors ruled a kingdom roughly equivalent to modern France, Switzerland, and part of western Germany.*

The early Frankish kings belonged to the Merovingian Dynasty, named for an ancestor called Meroweg. The Frankish churchman Gregory of Tours (c.538–594), who wrote the first history of the Merovingian kings, reported that they were known as "the long-haired kings" because they grew their hair over their shoulders. At the time long hair and beards were considered the mark of a barbarian; the Romanized citizens of Gaul were clean-shaven and wore their hair cropped. While the Merovingians clung to this link with their barbarian past, they were also ready to accommodate the customs of their Gallic subjects. Thus in 491 Clovis was baptized as a Catholic. His was probably a political rather than a religious conversion—to rule his new lands effectively, he needed to have the church on his side, since bishops played an important role in local administration.

▲ As this silver filigree earring suggests, a modest trade in luxury items survived in Frankish times, even though the great trade networks of the Roman era had been disrupted.

[Map]

- ✕ major battle
- → campaign by Clovis
- Frankish territory on accession of Clovis
- gains to Frankish Kingdom by Clovis
- gains by Clovis's sons to 561

0 — 300 km
0 — 200 mi

North Sea · Frisians · Saxons · *Elbe* · Cologne · *Rhine* · Thuringians · Tournai · Aix · AUSTRASIA · Cambrai · Trier · *Danube* · Rouen · Soissons 486 ✕ · *Seine* · Verdun · Worms · Paris · Strasbourg · Bavarians · Bretons · NEUSTRIA · Alemanni · Le Mans · Orléans · *Loire* · Salzburg · Tours · FRANKISH KINGDOM · Autun 532 ✕ · BURGUNDY · Vouillé 507 ✕ Poitiers · *ATLANTIC OCEAN* · AQUITAINE · Lyon · A L P S · OSTROGOTH KINGDOM · Milan · *Po* · Bordeaux · *Garonne* · *Rhône* · Genoa · GASCONY · Toulouse · Arles · PROVENCE · Basques · Narbonne · Marseille · P Y R E N E E S · *Mediterranean Sea* · Corsica · VISIGOTH KINGDOM · *Ebro* · Zaragoza · Barcelona

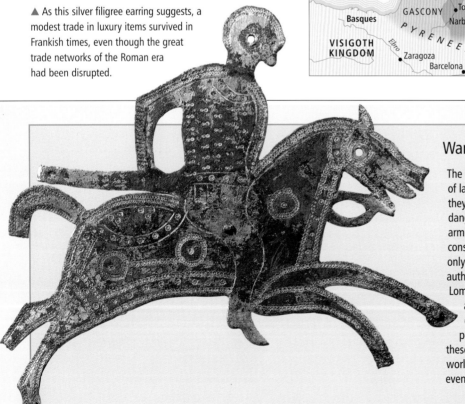

Warrior Kings

The collapse of the Roman Empire saw an end to the rule of law in Europe. Local kings tried to keep order as best they could, but for the majority of people life was more dangerous and uncertain than it had been when Roman armies guaranteed their security. Barbarian kings struggled constantly with rival monarchs and remained in power only for as long as they could win battles. To bolster their authority, they maintained groups of fighting men (like the Lombard cavalryman shown at left) in their households at their own expense. The soldiers had to be ready to do battle at any time and were given a share of any plunder that was looted while on campaign. It was from these household soldiers—known in the Anglo-Saxon world as housecarls—that the knights of medieval Europe eventually developed.

When Clovis died in his new capital of Paris in 511, his kingdom was divided between his four sons in accordance with Frankish tribal law. For most of the next 200 years the Frankish lands were separated into distinct kingdoms and were only rarely united under a single king. Rival heirs were constantly at war with one another, and assassinations were frequent. Real power passed from these *rois faineants* ("do-nothing kings") to the stewards of the royal household, known as "mayors of the palace."

By the mid-7th century the mayors of the palace were drawn exclusively from the Carolingian family (their name derives from Carolus, the Latin form of Charles). Outstanding among the Carolingian mayors was Charles Martel ("the Hammer"), who earned his nickname after defeating an Arab army near Tours in 732—a crucial victory that stemmed the advance of the forces of Islam into Christian Europe. Charles Martel actively promoted the mission of St. Boniface to convert the Germans to Christianity and was a great supporter of the church. He was succeeded by his son Pepin the Short. In 751 Pepin obtained permission from the Pope to depose the reigning Merovingian king, Childeric III, and contrived that an assembly of Frankish nobles should elect him king instead as the first ruler of a new Carolingian line.

◀ The Frankish Kingdom was largely the creation of Clovis, greatest of the Merovingian kings. Striking south from a homeland near the Rhine River, he conquered much of central and eastern France. Clovis made Paris his capital shortly before his death in 511.

▶ A medieval manuscript illustration shows Charles Martel confronting an Arab army at the Battle of Tours, just 100 miles (160 km) southwest of Paris. Charles's victory after six days of fighting stemmed the Arab advance into northern Europe.

🜲 **481** Clovis becomes king of the Franks, whose territory consists at the time of an area in present-day Belgium.

✕ **486** Clovis defeats Syragius, the last Roman general in Gaul, at Soissons in northern France.

✕ **507** Clovis drives the Visigoths from Aquitaine (southwest France).

🜲 **511** Clovis dies in his new capital of Paris; his kingdom is divided among his four sons.

🜲 **536** Burgundy (eastern France and Switzerland) becomes part of the Frankish Kingdom.

🜲 **537** The Franks win control of Provence (southeastern France).

🜲 **613** Lothair II reunites the Frankish Kingdom.

🜲 **638** Dagobert I, last of the great Merovingian kings, dies. He is succeeded by a series of short-lived kings in whose reigns power passes to the "mayors of the palace."

✕ **687** Pepin of Héristal, the Carolingian mayor of the palace, unites all the Frankish territories at the Battle of Tertry.

✕ **689** Pepin begins the conquest of the Frisians (present-day Netherlands).

🜲 **714** Charles Martel succeeds his father Pepin as mayor of the palace and effective ruler of the Franks.

✕ **732** Charles Martel wins a decisive victory over an Arab army at Tours in central France.

🜲 **741** Charles Martel dies and is succeeded by his son Pepin.

🜲 **754** Pepin is crowned by the pope in a ceremony at Reims, northern France, that formally affirms the Carolingian Dynasty as kings of the Franks.

550–600 A.D.

AMERICAS

556 The Mayan states of Caracol and Tikal go to war; Caracol finally wins the conflict in 562.

c.585 Some Early Classic Maya sites in the Petén lowlands of Guatemala are destroyed, perhaps as the result of drought.

c.600 The Huari Empire begins to expand north in the Andean highlands of southern Peru and west across the coastal plain.

EUROPE

c.550 The Slavs, farming peoples probably from present-day Belarus and Ukraine, migrate south across the Danube River.

552 A Byzantine army led by Narses expels the Ostrogoths from all of Italy south of the Po River (–554).

554 The armies of the Byzantine Emperor Justinian reconquer southern Spain from the Visigoths.

Crown of the Lombard King Agiluf

AFRICA

c.550 The Byzantine Empress Theodora sends missionaries to seek converts in North Africa.

c.550 The African Kingdom of Axum struggles with Sassanian Persia for control of Arabia (–574).

570 A Christian army from Axum attacks Mecca but is driven back.

WESTERN ASIA

554 The Sassanian rulers of Persia defeat the Ephthalite Huns, driving them beyond the Oxus (Amu Darya) River.

562 The Treaty of Edessa establishes temporary peace between the Byzantines and Sassanians. The Sassanians abandon claims to the Black Sea region in return for an annual payment of 30,000 gold pieces.

c.570 The Prophet Muhammad, founder of Islam, is born in Mecca into a merchant family.

572 The Byzantine Emperor Justin renews the war against the Sassanians.

SOUTH & CENTRAL ASIA

c.550 The Gurjaras establish a dynasty in northwest India.

553 The Juan-Juan—the confederation of Mongol tribes controlling the Silk Road—are overthrown by their Turkish subjects. One group, the Avars, migrates to eastern Europe.

572 The Turks establish a khanate (state) in Central Asia, which almost immediately splits into eastern and western divisions.

EAST ASIA & OCEANIA

c.550 The Kingdom of Chenla overthrows Funan in modern Cambodia and Thailand.

552 Buddhism is introduced to Japan.

557 The Northern Zhou Dynasty extends its power into the western and eastern parts of Wei, reuniting northern China (–577).

Silla was the easternmost of the three kingdoms set up in Korea in the mid-1st millennium A.D., when Chinese power in the peninsula came to an end. Thriving through its position on the China–Japan trade routes, it survived to the 10th century. The burial mounds of its kings can still be seen in their former capital of Kyongju (*left*).

High in the Peruvian Andes, the city of Huari housed perhaps 70,000 people, among them the potter who shaped this ceramic drinking vessel. From about the year 600 on, its people embarked on a series of successful military campaigns, building an empire that survived until the 9th century.

AMERICAS

EUROPE

✗ **559** The Byzantine general Belisarius defeats an army of Slavs and Huns at the gates of Constantinople.

✗ **c.560** A new wave of nomads, the Avars, enter eastern Europe from Central Asia; the Byzantines hire them to wipe out the last of the Huns.

☀ **563** St. Columba, an Irish monk, founds a monastery on the island of Iona off the Scottish west coast.

✗ **568** The Lombards, a Germanic people formerly allied to the Romans, invade northern Italy (–582) but fail to take control of Rome and Ravenna; they make their capital at Pavia.

✗ **571** The Visigoths recapture Córdoba in southern Spain.

✗ **c.580** The Avars overrun the Balkans and threaten the Byzantine Empire.

☀ **590** Gregory I (the Great) is elected pope.

📖 **591** Gregory of Tours completes *The History of the Franks*.

✗ **592** The Byzantine Emperor Maurice campaigns against the Avars in the Balkans (–602).

☀ **597** Pope Gregory I sends St. Augustine at the head of a mission to Britain to convert the Anglo-Saxons.

AFRICA

☀ **c.570** The Nubian Kingdom of Makurra (in today's Sudan) is converted to Christianity.

☀ **c.580** The missionary Longinus similarly converts Makurra's neighbor, the Kingdom of Alwa.

WESTERN ASIA

✗ **574** Having ravaged Syria, Khusrow I of Persia drives the Axumites out of Yemen in southern Arabia and joins it to the Sassanian Empire.

👑 **579** Death of Khusrow I; he is succeeded by Hormazd I.

✗ **589** The Sassanian general Bahram invades Colchis on the Black Sea but is defeated by a Byzantine army near the Araxes River.

✗ **589** Hormazd is murdered. His son Khusrow II succeeds him.

👑 **590–591** Bahram overthrows Khusrow II of Persia, who is later restored with the help of the Byzantine Emperor Maurice. Bahram takes refuge with the Turks but is murdered by them.

SOUTH & CENTRAL ASIA

👑 **c.575** In India the Pallava warrior dynasty extends its control of the southern Deccan as far as the Kaveri River.

✗ **c.590** The western Turks threaten the frontiers of the Persian Empire.

✷ **c.600** Indian mathematicians have developed the decimal point and the concept of zero by this date.

EAST ASIA & OCEANIA

✗ **562** The state of Silla expels the Japanese from Korea.

✗ **581** Yang Jian overthrows the Northern Zhou Dynasty and founds the Sui Dynasty; he rules as Sui Wendi.

👑 **589** Sui Wendi reunifies China.

👑 **593** In Japan Prince Shotoku adopts Chinese models of government; he introduces Chinese craftsmen to the Japanese court (–622).

👑 **c.600** A Thai kingdom is established in Yunnan (southern China).

Chinese sculptures of two Sui Dynasty officials.

550–600 A.D.

TEOTIHUACÁN

IN THE MID-1ST MILLENNIUM A.D. *a city the size of early imperial Rome flourished in the highlands of central Mexico. Its population of perhaps 200,000 people made it one of the world's largest metropolises at the time. Yet its inhabitants knew neither iron- nor bronzeworking and had no writing. As a result, even the city's name has not been recorded. Today it is known by the title given to it by later peoples, who marveled at its ruins more than 500 years after its final destruction by fire. They called it Teotihuacán, "place of the gods."*

▲ Lying about 30 miles (50 km) north of modern Mexico City, Teotihuacán was the biggest city in the Americas in its day. This stone head decorated the Pyramid of the Feathered Serpent, a shrine built over the graves of at least 137 individuals, many of whom are thought to have been offered as sacrificial victims at its dedication.

The Valley of Mexico is a 3,000-square-mile (8,000-sq.-km) basin 5,000 feet (1,500 m) up in the mountains of central Mexico. Despite its temperate highland climate, well suited for the growing of maize (corn), the valley had been a cultural backwater until the final centuries B.C. Then, suddenly, its population started to grow.

One reason may have been improved agricultural techniques: The local peasants began terracing their fields and digging irrigation canals. Another was the discovery of one of Central America's best deposits of obsidian nearby. This volcanic glass can be flaked to produce a razor-sharp edge, making it invaluable for the manufacture of tools and weapons among people who, like the Teotihuacans, had no iron.

In time a town grew up that by the year 100 A.D. already housed perhaps 60,000 people. Unusually for the time, it was laid out on a grid pattern, with a dead-straight central thoroughfare that was lined with plazas, palaces, and monuments. The greatest of them were two towering pyramids, known to later peoples as the Pyramid of the Sun (see box) and the Pyramid of the Moon.

Beyond the main axis residential quarters spread out across the plain. Archaeological excavations have shown that the city's ruling class lived in spacious villas with painted walls built around central courtyards. Most citizens, however, inhabited single-story apartment complexes, each the size of a city block, divided into warrens of rooms often no bigger

▶ Teotihuacán's influence radiated outward from the Valley of Mexico—the area where Mexico City now lies. Traders from the city penetrated the Zapotec heartland around Monte Albán and also the Mayan lands of the Petén rainforest and the Yucatán Peninsula.

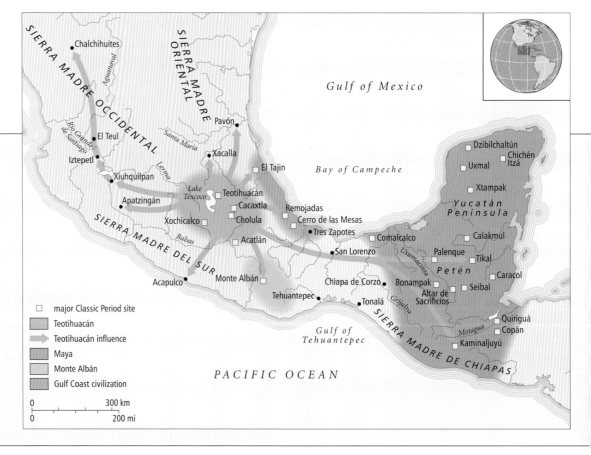

Gulf of Mexico

Bay of Campeche

Gulf of Tehuantepec

PACIFIC OCEAN

SIERRA MADRE OCCIDENTAL

SIERRA MADRE ORIENTAL

SIERRA MADRE DEL SUR

SIERRA MADRE DE CHIAPAS

Yucatán Peninsula

Petén

Chalchihuites • Pavón • El Teul • Iztepetl • Xiuhquilpan • Apatzingán • Xochicalco • Acapulco • Monte Albán • Tehuantepec • Tonalá • Acatlán • San Lorenzo • Chiapa de Corzo • Bonampak • Altar de Sacrificios • Seibal • Caracol • Tikal • Palenque • Comalcalco • Calakmúl • Xtampak • Uxmal • Chichén Itzá • Dzibilchaltún • Quiriguá • Copán • Kaminaljuyú • Tres Zapotes • Cerro de las Mesas • Remojadas • Cacaxtla • Cholula • Teotihuacán • Xacalla • El Tajin

Lake Texcoco

Rio Grande de Santiago • Aguanaval • Santa Maria • Lerma • Balsas • Usumacinta • Grijalva • Motagua

major Classic Period site
Teotihuacán
Teotihuacán influence
Maya
Monte Albán
Gulf Coast civilization

0 _____ 300 km
0 _____ 200 mi

The Pyramid of the Sun

The Pyramid of the Sun was the largest of Teotihuacán's monuments; at 738 feet (225 m) square, its base was almost as big as that of Egypt's Great Pyramid, although it stood less than half as high. In its final form it rose in four steps to a flat summit, where a shrine once stood. The tradition that the pyramid was dedicated to the sun dates from Aztec times; in reality, no one knows for sure what was worshiped there. A clue to its original purpose, however, turned up in 1971, when archaeologists discovered a tunnel leading into its depths. At its end was a cave artificially enlarged into the shape of a clover leaf. Scholars have speculated that it represented a "Place of Emergence"—a cave of a type familiar in Central American mythology, from which tribal ancestors were believed to have emerged in the distant past.

than closets. The residents supported themselves by agriculture, cultivating crops on small parcels in the surrounding countryside, and by industry that capitalized on local materials: There were more than 400 obsidian workshops in the city as well as over 200 potteries. Trade was also important, for merchants carried the goods produced in Teotihuacán's workshops all over Mexico.

By 450 A.D. Teotihuacán was at its peak. Then, around 650, disaster struck. For unknown reasons the temples and monuments at its heart were put to the torch, and in the ensuing decades the city's population collapsed, leaving nothing but ruins. Historians speculate that the metropolis may have foundered as a result of its own success; the burgeoning population may have exhausted the wood and other resources of the surrounding area. But whether the final destruction was accomplished by outside invaders or by Teotihuacán's own restive citizens remains a mystery.

Teotihuacán's builders did not date their monuments as the Maya of southern Mexico and Guatemala did, so all dates for its history can only be approximate.

🌊 **c.0 A.D.** Teotihuacán starts to emerge as an important urban center in the Valley of Mexico.

🌊 **c.100** By this date the city already covers more than 2 square miles (5 sq. km).

☀ **c.150** Work gets under way on the Pyramid of the Sun, the city's largest building and one of the biggest in the Americas.

🌊 **c.250** By this time Teotihuacán has developed into a major metropolis, laid out on a grid pattern with residential blocks surrounding an avenue of palaces and temples.

🌊 **c.300** The city of Teotihuacán is by now the hub of the most powerful state in central Mexico.

🌊 **c.400** A Zapotec quarter develops in the city, inhabited by traders and craftsmen who produce pottery and utensils in the Zapotec style, use Zapotec characters for writing, and bury their dead in the manner favored at the Zapotec capital of Monte Albán.

🌊 **c.450** Teotihuacán is at the peak of its influence and power; it has an estimated population of 200,000 people and covers an area of 8 square miles (20 sq. km).

✕ **c.650** Teotihuacán is sacked and burned by unknown assailants.

🌊 **c.700** Cholula takes Teotihuacán's place as the major urban center in the Valley of Mexico. Its central pyramid will in time rival the Pyramid of the Sun in size.

600–650 A.D.

AMERICAS

🏛 **c.600** Perhaps on account of an El Niño-influenced drought, the Moche people forsake their settlements on Peru's coastal plain, founding a new capital farther to the north.

🏛 **c.600** The Tiahuanaco civilization, based around Lake Titicaca in the Andean altiplano (high plateau), is at its peak. Its prosperity is built on irrigated agriculture, copper-working, and trade.

⚙ **c.600** In the American Southwest the Anasazi—successors of the earlier Basketmaker Culture—begin the transition from small, sunken pithouses to aboveground, multiroomed pueblos.

EUROPE

After the collapse of city life following the withdrawal of Roman troops in 407, England gradually returned to some kind of order in the 7th century. The land was no longer united, as it had been under the Romans; now it was divided into half a dozen separate kingdoms ruled by Anglo-Saxon kings (one such is shown with his council at left). The native people mostly integrated with the settlers, although Celtic groups held out in the southwest and in Wales.

🏛 **602** The Byzantine army commander Phokas becomes emperor in what amounts to a military coup.

🏛 **610** With Byzantium weakened by war with Sassanian Persia, Heraclius, governor of Carthage, displaces Phokas as emperor.

AFRICA

🏛 **c.600** In West Africa the Kingdom of Ghana emerges to the north of modern-day Ghana.

🏛 **c.600** As climate change increases aridity, the Sahara spreads slowly south.

WESTERN ASIA

⚔ **614** Jerusalem falls into Sassanian hands. The "True Cross" of Jesus is seized and carried off to Persia.

⚔ **620** Khusrow II is captured and executed by the Byzantine Emperor Heraclius, heralding the decline of Persia's Sassanian Dynasty.

🏛 **c.620** The Turkic Khazars establish an empire in the northern Caucasus.

☀ **622** The year of the *hijra*, or Hejira— the flight of Muhammad and his followers from Mecca to Medina.

⚔ **627** Byzantine armies defeat the Sassanians at Nineveh, Iraq.

⚔ **629** Heraclius retakes Egypt, Syria, and Palestine for Byzantium but almost immediately faces a new threat from the forces of Islam.

☀ **632** The Prophet Muhammad dies. His succession by Abu Bakr stores up trouble for the future.

⚔ **633** Arab forces invade Sassanian territories.

⚔ **635** The Arabs take Damascus from the Byzantines.

⚔ **636** Byzantine forces are decisively defeated by the Arabs at the Battle of Yarmuk in Jordan.

⚔ **637** Arab forces smash Sassanian power for good at the Battle of Qadisiya, following which the dynasty's capital at Ctesiphon (Iraq) quickly falls.

⚔ **638** The Arabs take Jerusalem.

SOUTH & CENTRAL ASIA

🏛 **606** The "Age of Small Kingdoms" comes to an end with the accession of Harshavardhana; over the next four decades he will build an impressive Buddhist empire in north and east India.

🏛 **608** Pulakesin II, greatest ruler of the Chalukya Dynasty, comes to the throne (–642). Much of south India will eventually be united under Chalukya rule.

7th-century Tibetan Buddhist decoration.

EAST ASIA & OCEANIA

🏛 **c.600** The Champa civilization comes of age in central Vietnam, its kings promoting Hindu religion and a highly Indianized culture.

⚙ **605** A four-year program begins in China to build the 1,200-mile (2,000-km) Grand Canal.

⚙ **612** The first inscription in the Khmer language at Angkor in Cambodia dates from this year.

AMERICAS

✺ **c.600** Long past its prime, the Hopewell Culture of the American Midwest fades further as communities are drawn south by the attractions of a corn-based agricultural lifestyle.

👑 **c.615** Classic Mayan civilization reaches a peak in Palenque with the accession of 12-year-old King Pacal ("Shield"). His 68-year reign will see the city become one of Mesoamerica's finest.

👑 **c.640** The Mayan city-states of Dos Pilas and Aguateca are founded by Ruler 1, a member of Tikal's ruling family.

EUROPE

✗ **c.615** By now the Anglo-Saxon conquest of England is largely complete.

👑 **623** The Frankish merchant Samo brings Slavic Czechs and Slovaks together to fight the Avars. The union breaks up after his death in 659.

✗ **626** Constantinople resists a siege by the Avars, Slavs, and Persians.

👑 **c.630** East Anglia emerges as foremost in the heptarchy (literally "rule of seven") of Anglo-Saxon kingdoms of England. The others are Kent, Wessex, Essex, Sussex, Mercia, and Northumbria.

☀ **635** St. Aidan founds a monastery on Lindisfarne, off the coast of Northumbria.

👑 **641** Heraclius dies, leaving the Byzantine Empire beset by barbarian tribes from the north and west, Arabs from the south, and Persians from the east.

AFRICA

👑 **c.600** The Zhagawa people settle by Lake Chad; their descendants will found the Kanem Kingdom there.

👑 **c.600** Axum goes into steady decline, Persian conquests having disrupted its trade routes.

✗ **639** Arab armies conquer Egypt (–642).

WESTERN ASIA

✗ **643** Arab victory at Nehavend, in the Zagros Mountains, effectively ends Sassanian resistance in Iran.

👑 **645** The Umayyad caliphs establish their capital in Damascus.

✗ **649** The Arabs take the Sassanian city of Istakhr, massacring its inhabitants, and desecrate the ruins of the ancient Achaemenid capital of Persepolis nearby.

The Sassanian Dynasty, one of whose kings is shown hunting boar at left, ruled Persia for more than 400 years after overthrowing the Parthian Empire in 224 A.D. In that time its rulers revived much of the glory of the Old Persian Empire of Cyrus the Great. However, ongoing warfare with their Byzantine neighbors sapped their resources, and they quickly fell victim to the forces of the new faith of Islam in the decade after 633.

SOUTH & CENTRAL ASIA

👑 **c.609** King Songtsen Gampo comes to power in Tibet. His reign will see the introduction of Buddhism to the country and its establishment as the official state religion.

✗ **620** Pulakesin II's forces stem the southward expansion of Harshavardhana's empire.

✗ **632** Pulakesin is defeated by the Pallava King Narasimha Varman.

📖 **646** Chinese monk Xuanzang publishes his *Records of the Western World*, an account of a trip to India.

👑 **647** Harshavardhana dies heirless, and his empire dies with him.

EAST ASIA & OCEANIA

👑 **618** Usurping his Sui cousin, Li Yuan seizes power in China, founding the Tang Dynasty and ruling under the name of Gaozu.

👑 **626** Li Yuan's son takes power as the Emperor Taizong. The key achievement of his 23-year rule will be the quelling of nomadic tribes to the north and the opening up of trade routes to western Asia.

👑 **646** A series of measures taken by the Japanese Emperor Kotoku, the Taika or "Great Change" represents a concerted attempt to remodel Japanese society along Chinese lines.

600–650 A.D.

MUHAMMAD AND ISLAM

▲ Shown here in a 19th-century woodcut, Muhammad was both a visionary prophet and a charismatic leader. In 627 he confirmed his authority by defending his adopted home city of Medina against rivals from Mecca in a two-week struggle known as the Battle of the Ditch.

FOR CENTURIES THE ARABIAN PENINSULA *seemed to be a backwater, its inhabitants all but forgotten by the rest of humanity. Wild horsemen and camel drivers, the Arabs emerged from the depths of the desert only on occasional raids against outlying settlements before returning to the desert from which they came. One man, Muhammad, would change all that, giving his people first a spiritual and then a military mission. By the end of the 7th century the Arabs had made themselves the masters of vast territories and carried the Muslim message through much of the world.*

"The distant Arabs dwelling in the desert … know neither overseers nor officials." This was the disdainful view of Sargon II of Assyria around 700 B.C. No anthropologist, the emperor overlooked the perfection with which the Arabs' lifestyle as nomadic camel herders was adapted to one of the world's most hostile environments. Yet it was true that they lived a marginal existence, far beyond the reach of what was generally recognized as civilization. A thousand years later it was still the same. To the east the Iran-based empire of the Sassanians flourished, to the north were the Greco-Roman realms of Byzantium, but the Arabs stood apart, as though history had passed them by.

All this would change, however, when in 610 a middle-aged businessman in the city of Mecca started seeing visions. In the years that followed, the Angel Gabriel appeared to Muhammad again and again,

dictating to him the word of Allah—God. The name for the new religion, Islam, meant "surrender" to the divine will: It resembled Judaism and Christianity in many respects, notably its monotheism—worship of a single deity.

Inspired by religious zeal and a message of charity for the poor, Muhammad and his followers could not help but find themselves at odds with the Quraysh, Mecca's wealthy elite. In 622 they left for the neighboring city of Medina. Relations with Medina's three tribes of Jews were good at first, although as hostilities with Mecca escalated, they deteriorated, the Muslims fearing that the Jews might make alliance with their Arab enemies.

In time the Muslims gained control of Mecca, and their victory marked the start of one of the most amazing campaigns of conquest the world has ever

The Kaaba

Mecca had been a holy place for Arabs long before Muhammad was born. For centuries they had flocked to the city to venerate the Kaaba, a shrine enclosing a sacred black stone fallen from heaven—in scientific terms a meteorite. Muhammad's falling out with the city's rulers owed much to his indignation at the way in which they exploited the pilgrims who came to worship there. Yet, radical as he was in rejecting paganism, Muhammad was also a traditionalist, and he made the Kaaba the object of a specifically Islamic pilgrimage. To this day all Muslims are expected at some stage in their lifetime to make the *hajj*—the journey to Mecca to walk around the Kaaba—and each summer crowds fill the vast shrine that now surrounds it *(right)*.

☀ **c.570** Birth of the Prophet Muhammad in Mecca, Arabia.

☀ **c.610** Muhammad's divine mission begins with the first appearance to him of the Archangel Gabriel.

☀ **622** The *hijra*, or "emigration": Muhammad and his followers leave Mecca for the city of Yathrib, since known as Medina, "city of the Prophet," in his honor. The *hijra* marks the start of the Muslim calendar; all dates are calculated from this year.

✗ **624** Muslims defeat the Meccans at the Battle of Badr.

✗ **625** Muhammad's forces suffer a setback when they are defeated at Uhud.

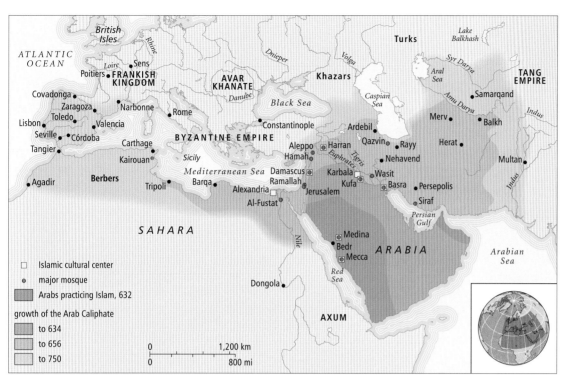

◀ From a heartland near the Red Sea Islam first spread over the Arabian Peninusula, then the Near East and Persia. By 750 Muslims ruled lands stretching from the Indus River to Spain. However, the Byzantine Empire succeeded in checking Islam's progress along the Mediterranean's northern shores.

Legend on map:
- ☐ Islamic cultural center
- ◉ major mosque
- Arabs practicing Islam, 632
- growth of the Arab Caliphate
  - to 634
  - to 656
  - to 750

0 — 1,200 km
0 — 800 mi

▼ The chief vehicle for Islam's message is the Koran, which Muslims hold to be the word of God as revealed to Muhammad over a 20-year period. This manuscript fragment dates back to the time of the Abbasid Dynasty in the 8th or 9th century.

seen. By the time the Prophet died in 632, to be controversially succeeded by his father-in-law, the Arabs had already carried the word by force of arms—and inspiration—through much of West Asia. Although their warlike nature had always been recognized, the Arabs had hitherto been dismissed as little more than raiders, a mere nuisance: Now, however, their aggression was channeled by a passionate faith. Within a few decades these forgotten desert nomads made much of the known world their own, building an Islamic empire that stretched all the way from the edges of India to southern Spain.

✕ **627** A Meccan army is turned back from Medina at the Battle of the Ditch. After the victory Muhammad attacks the city's chief Jewish tribe, suspected of conspiring with the Meccans; the men are massacred, the women and children enslaved.

✕ **630** Meccans surrender their city, and the Kaaba, to the Muslims. Muhammad launches a raid through northern Arabia to the borders of Byzantine Syria.

🏛 **632** Death of Muhammad. A meeting of elders elects his father-in-law, Abu Bakr, to inherit his authority as *khalifah*, or caliph ("successor"), rather than his cousin and son-in-law Ali ibn Abi Talib. The decision will have enormous implications for subsequent Islamic history.

✕ **634** Battle of Ajnadyn brings victory over Byzantine forces in Syria.

🏛 **634** Umar ibn al-Khattab (Omar I) becomes second caliph.

✕ **636** Victory over Byzantines at the Yarmuk River brings all Syria under Muslim control.

✕ **637** The Persians are defeated at the Battle of Qadisiya, opening the way into Iraq and the Sassanian heartland of Iran.

✕ **641** The Arabs take Cairo, Egypt; the Mediterranean port of Alexandria falls in the following year.

🏛 **644** Umar is assassinated. His successor as caliph, Uthman, is most famous for having gathered Muhammad's various visionary pronouncements into a single book, the Koran.

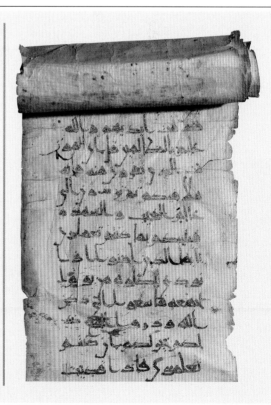

650–700 A.D.

AMERICAS

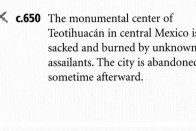

✗ **c.650** The monumental center of Teotihuacán in central Mexico is sacked and burned by unknown assailants. The city is abandoned sometime afterward.

Detail from a painted ceramic vase found at the Mayan city of Tikal.

EUROPE

✗ **c.650** Visigoth rule in Spain is increasingly riven by internal faction fighting.

☀ **664** The Synod of Whitby, a church council held in northern England, establishes papal control over the English church, rejecting practices favored in the Celtic churches of Wales, Ireland, and Scotland.

✗ **c.670** Bulgar raiders of Turkic origin move into the Balkan Peninsula.

❀ **678** Byzantine forces use "Greek fire" — a flammable mixture of sulfur, naphtha, and quicklime fired from bronze tubes—to end a five-year blockade of Constantinople, marking a first significant setback for Islam's forces.

AFRICA

👑 **c.650** The centuries-long Bantu migration from West Africa ends, with Bantu speakers now found through east and southern Africa.

☀ **c.650** Islamic influences start to spread down the East African coast through what is already longstanding maritime trade.

✗ **651** The Arab rulers of Egypt launch their first expedition against the Christian Nubian kingdoms of Alwa and Makurra.

WESTERN ASIA

☀ **651** Caliph Uthman brings Muhammad's teachings together to form a single sacred volume, the Koran.

✗ **654** Having taken Armenia from Byzantium, Arab forces turn westward into the empire's heartland in Anatolia (Turkey).

👑 **656** Uthman's assassination precipitates the outbreak of Islam's first civil war.

👑 **661** The civil war comes to an end with the murder of Ali, the Prophet's cousin and son-in-law. The victorious Umayyads establish their capital in Damascus.

✗ **680** The sons of Ali (Hasan and Husayn) and their supporters are massacred at Karbala, Iraq.

✗ **683** The death of Umayyad Caliph Yazid I triggers a second Islamic Civil War.

👑 **692** Abd al-Malik succeeds in holding on to the caliphate for the Umayyads, although his ruthlessness will be resented by Shiites for generations.

SOUTH & CENTRAL ASIA

👑 **c.650** The disintegration of Harshavardhana's empire brings a return to regionalism and local cultures in India.

☀ **651** The Arab capture of Merv, in modern Turkmenistan, brings Islam to Central Asia.

👑 **659** Tang Dynasty victories against the Turks extend Chinese control of the Silk Road westward.

Earthenware figurine of a dancer from Tang Dynasty China.

EAST ASIA & OCEANIA

☀ **c.651** Islam is brought to China for the first time by Arab traders.

👑 **653** The first known Tang Dynasty law code dates from this year; its influence will linger for centuries.

👑 **657** Jayavarman I founds the dynasty that (in a century or so) will rule the powerful and prosperous Khmer Empire in Cambodia.

👑 **682** "Ruler A" comes to power in the Mayan city of Tikal, Guatemala: nothing is known of him except that he seems to have transformed the flagging fortunes of his state.

✕ **695** Tikal finally defeats its northerly neighbor and longstanding enemy Calakmul. The city enjoys a boom in commerce and a renaissance in art and sculpture, its population rising to about 50,000 people.

👑 **695** The Mayan city of Copán, Honduras, begins its golden age with the accession of Waxaklajuun Ub'aah K'awiil.

AMERICAS

👑 **681** The Bulgars sign a treaty agreeing to help protect Constantinople against Slavic raiders. In return the Byzantines recognize the new Kingdom of Bulgaria.

👑 **685** The Byzantine Emperor Constantine IV negotiates a treaty with the Arabs establishing a firm frontier between the Byzantine and Arab spheres.

👑 **687** The people of Venice, Italy, organize their city as a republic, with an elected "doge," or leader.

☀ **c.690** English missionaries are at work spreading Christianity in Scandinavia and the Netherlands.

✕ **700** The Balkans are overrun by Avar and Slavic tribes.

EUROPE

✕ **670** Uqba ibn Nafi leads Arab armies into what is now Tunisia, launching a new campaign in the Maghreb—western North Africa.

👑 **675** Kairouan, in modern Tunisia, is founded as a base for the conquest of the Maghreb.

✕ **698** After several years' intermittent assault Arab forces take the ancient city of Carthage.

AFRICA

☀ **692** The Dome of the Rock is completed in Jerusalem.

👑 **692** Abd al-Malik introduces new coinage with Koranic verses for use throughout the Islamic world. To the disapproval of many purists the caliph's vision of Islam transcends the religious sphere to comprise a whole new social and economic order.

The Dome of the Rock in Jerusalem is one of Islam's holiest shrines. Commissioned by the Umayyad Caliph Abd al-Malik in 687, it was completed five years later. Inside its octagonal walls lies the rock on which Abraham was said to have offered his son Isaac to God; according to Muslim tradition, the Prophet Muhammad, founder of Islam, ascended to heaven from the spot.

WESTERN ASIA

✕ **664** The Arab advance reaches Kabul in what is now Afghanistan.

✕ **670** Sustained Tibetan attacks expel Tang forces from the Tarim Basin in present-day western China. The victory cuts off China from westward trade.

✕ **674** The Arabs reach the Indus River in modern Pakistan.

✕ **692** Tang forces, with their Turkic allies, seize back the Tarim Basin from the Tibetans.

SOUTH & CENTRAL ASIA

✕ **660** The southern Korean Kingdom of Silla invades neighboring Paekche.

✕ **668** Silla attacks its other Korean rival, Koguryo, then imposes peace on the peninsula.

✕ **676** Having established its dominance throughout Korea, Silla drives Chinese forces out of the peninsula.

👑 **690** Wu Zetian takes power as China's first and only empress.

📖 **699** Birth of Wang Wei, Buddhist scholar and one of China's greatest painters and poets.

EAST ASIA & OCEANIA

650–700 A.D.

SUNNIS AND SHIITES

EXPLOSIVE IN ITS IMPACT, *Islam seemed to carry all before it in the 7th century when the power of faith was backed up by force of arms. The speed and stamina of its warriors' horses, their skill in the saddle, their military prowess, and their sense of destiny—all conspired to make the Arab advance irresistible. Yet as time went on, there would increasingly be wars within Islam itself, creating tensions that would ultimately split the entire Muslim community.*

▲ Islam may have begun life as a religion of the Arabian desert, but in a very short time its adherents brought most of the great cities of the Middle East under its sway. This mosaic townscape comes from the Great Mosque in Damascus, capital of Syria.

Najaf

Some 80 miles (130 km) south of Baghdad, Iraq, stands the sacred shrine of Mashad Gharwah, reputed to be the burial place of Ali, Muhammad's son-in-law and would-be successor. The story goes that having been mortally wounded by his murderers, he asked his followers to tie him to the back of a camel and turn the beast loose: Wherever it stopped to rest, there they should build his tomb. Today the site is one of the holiest shrines of Shia Islam: Many thousands make the pilgrimage to it each year. An idea of its importance to Shiites can be had from the fact that a visit in turn to Najaf and to Karbala (where Ali's sons Hasan and the martyred Husayn lie buried) is held by many to be spiritually equivalent to the *hajj*, or pilgrimage to Mecca.

---

632 Muhammad dies, and Abu Bakr, his father-in-law, is elected to succeed him as first of the *ar-Rashidun*, or "rightly guided" caliphs. In choosing him over the Prophet's son-in-law, Ali ibn Abi Talib, the Islamic elders are sowing the seeds of future strife.

656 Ali eventually becomes caliph, but his succession is disputed. Outbreak of first civil war between Ali and dissident Muslims led by Muawiya, governor of Syria.

661 The war ends with Ali's murder and Muawiya's recognition as caliph. His Umayyad descendants will hold sway over the Islamic world for the next 90 years.

680 The conflict passes down a generation as Husayn, son of Ali, attempts to seize power from Muawiya's heir, Yazid. He and his supporters are massacred at Karbala, Iraq.

683 Yazid dies, and a second civil war breaks out. Power passes eventually to Abd al-Malik, who reasserts Umayyad power at the cost of permanently alienating his Shiite opponents.

692 The Dome of the Rock, Jerusalem, is completed on the spot from which the Prophet is reputed to have ascended to heaven.

706 Construction of the Umayyad Mosque, Damascus, begins: It still stands as one of the architectural wonders of the world.

711 The first Muslim raids across the Straits of Gibraltar into southern Spain take place.

715 The Arab conquest of the Iberian Peninsula (Spain and Portugal) is completed.

732 The Arab advance into Europe is finally checked outside Tours in central France.

Although it was a moment of great sadness, the Prophet's death in the June of 632 was a time too of considerable hope and expectation. The visions Muhammad had experienced had already formed the basis of a significant religion, with adherents and territories through much of Arabia and beyond. The Prophet himself had already mounted expeditions in Byzantine Syria—perhaps sensing that a common military project was the best way of uniting his people's traditionally quarrelsome tribal factions.

But first of all it had to be decided who was to succeed the Prophet as leader of the Muslims: Muhammad had left no son. The seeds of future division were sown when a meeting of elders chose Abu Bakr, the Prophet's father-in-law, as *khalifah*, or caliph—a title that implied both spiritual authority and political rule. In making this choice, they passed over Muhammad's cousin and son-in-law, Ali, whose moral rigidity and religious fervor seem to have caused the elders some nervousness.

In a series of civil wars fought over the next 53 years, first Ali himself and then his sons attempted to wrest back the succession that they saw as rightly theirs. Over time doctrinal differences would also develop to further separate the rival groups. Those who followed Abu Bakr and the succession of "rightly guided" caliphs who came after him called themselves Sunni Muslims, because they followed the *sunnah*, or "customs," established by the Prophet. Shiites argued that this succession had been corrupted from the start, and that Islamic tradition should have flowed directly through the person of Ali to the line of imams, or "teachers," who came after him.

In 680 Ali's son Husayn and a small band of partisans were killed near Karbala in what is now Iraq as they traveled to join rebels in Iran pressing his

claim to the caliphate. The deaths gave Shiism its first martyrs and, although a defeat, lent the movement a new impetus. By 750 the Sunnis of the Umayyad Dynasty had been swept away by the Abbasid caliphs, based in Baghdad. Although their advent was not, strictly speaking, a Shiite revolution—Shiism recognized no rule higher than that of its own imams—the Abbasids could hardly have prevailed without the backing of the Shiite scholars. Divisions between Sunni and Shia Islam have persisted to this day, a source of distrust and at times of open warfare.

▲ In a 19th-century painting pilgrims commemorating the martyrdom of Muhammad's grandson Husayn approach the town of Karbala. Husayn, a claimant to the caliphate, was killed nearby by troops sent by the Caliph Yazid in 680. The town remains one of Shiite Islam's holiest sites.

〰 **747** The province of Khorasan, Persia, rebels against Umayyad rule, the first open display of resistance to a dynasty whose legitimacy is increasingly coming into question.

〰 **750** Muhammad ibn Ali ibn al-Abbas, a descendant of Ali, mounts a successful revolt against the Umayyads. He establishes his own Abbasid Dynasty, which reigns throughout the Middle East and North Africa (the Maghreb). The last Umayyads hold out in al-Andalus, southern Spain—the region now known as Andalusia—which they make their kingdom.

〰 **762** Foundation of Baghdad by al-Mansur. The new Abbasid capital becomes the center of a thriving commercial empire, with trade (through the port of Basra) to China and East Africa.

📖 **786** The accession of Harun al-Rashid ushers in a golden age, with astonishing achievements in art, literature, music, mathematics, medicine, and science.

〰 **913** Abbasid power sustains a major blow when Persia is overrun by the Buyids, an alliance of nomadic peoples from the southern shores of the Caspian Sea.

〰 **930** Rebels sack Mecca, confirming a weakening of Abbasid power that has been becoming more evident for decades. The dynasty's difficulties are compounded by the westward advance of the Seljuk Turks from Central Asia.

〰 **945** The Buyids conquer Iraq, the heartland of Abbasid rule.

☀ **969** A North African tribe, the Fatimids, seizes power in Egypt on its way to a wider dominance in the Islamic world. A Shiite group, they see their descent from Ali as being doubly sacred, through his relationship both with the Prophet himself and with his daughter, Fatima.

700–750 A.D.

AMERICAS

- **c.700** Monte Albán, the major Zapotec center in the Oaxaca Valley, is in decline by this time.

- **c.700** The Huari Empire conquers the Moche state of northern Peru.

- **735** The Mayan city of Seibal is conquered by Dos Pilas.

- **738** King Canac Sky of the Mayan city of Quiriguá rebels against King 18 Rabbit of Copán, whom he captures and beheads.

EUROPE

Icons like this image of the Virgin and Child from the Church of the Nativity in Bethlehem were at the center of a controversy that split the Byzantine Empire for more than a century from 726 on. In that year Emperor Leo III condemned the veneration of the much-loved images as a form of idolatry. Orthodox Christians remained deeply divided on the issue until 843, when the worship of holy images was officially restored.

- **c.710** Willibrord, an Anglo-Saxon monk, leads a mission to the pagan Danes.

- **711** An Arab army invades and conquers Spain as far as the Pyrenees (–715).

- **718** An Arab force fails to capture Constantinople.

- **718** The Danes build an earthen frontier in the south to defend their kingdom from the Saxons.

AFRICA

- **702** Berber resistance to Arab rule ends when the rebels' leader, Kahina "the Prophetess," is defeated and commits suicide.

- **706** Arabic becomes the official language of Egypt.

- **709** Arabs conquer Tangier.

- **725** Egypt's Christian Copts revolt unsuccessfully against Islamic rule.

WESTERN ASIA

- **c.715** The Islamic caliphate, ruled from Damascus, now extends from the Indus region to North Africa and Spain—the largest empire the world has yet seen.

- **720–724** Quarrels between Yemenites and Modharites—also known as southern and northern Arabs—spread through the Islamic world.

- **747** A major rebellion in the province of Khorasan is sparked by discontent among new converts to Islam who do not enjoy the same tax privileges as Arabs.

- **749** The rebels proclaim as caliph Abu-al Abbas, a member of the Abbasid family descended from Abbas, Muhammad's uncle.

SOUTH & CENTRAL ASIA

- **c.700** The Pallava rulers of south India build a temple complex at Mahabalipuram, with many fine rock-cut monuments.

The Shore Temple, Mahabalipuram, India.

- **c.700** Persian Zoroastrians take refuge from the advance of Islam by fleeing to western India, where they settle and become known as Parsis.

EAST ASIA & OCEANIA

- **c.700** China enjoys a period of great artistic creativity under the Tang emperors; poetry, figure painting, and pottery all reach high levels of attainment.

- **708** Official coinage is issued in Japan for the first time.

- **710** The Yamato emperors of Japan make a permanent capital at Nara.

- **712** Japan's oldest extant book, the *Kojiki*, which records the succession of Japan's ruling dynasty from mythical times, is written, employing Chinese characters.

⊕ **c.750** The Great Pyramid at Cholula in the Valley of Mexico is enlarged.

A stele from Quiriguá in what is now Guatemala depicts a Mayan king.

✕ **718** A Christian army defeats an Arab army at Covadonga in the mountains of Asturias in northern Spain.

☀ **719** Pope Gregory II commissions St. Boniface, an Anglo-Saxon originally named Wynfrith, to convert the Germans.

☀ **726** The Iconoclast Controversy (over the worship of images) causes a deep breach between the Orthodox and Roman churches.

✕ **732** An Arab army from Spain advances far into France but is turned back at Tours by a Frankish army led by Charles Martel.

📖 **735** Bede, chronicler of the English church, dies in his monastery at Jarrow in northern England.

🌊 **741** Charles Martel dies.

☀ **744** St. Boniface founds an abbey at Fulda in Germany that will become a great center of learning.

🌊 **750** The Lombards capture Ravenna, ending Byzantine power in central Italy.

⊕ **734** Ali Ubaida leads an expedition across the Sahara in search of gold.

✕ **739** Maisara leads an uprising of Berbers and followers of the Kharijite sect of Islam against Arab rule in Morocco.

✕ **742** The Kharijite and Berber revolt is suppressed.

The caliphs of the Abbasid Dynasty, which replaced the Umayyads from 750, ruled much of the Islamic world from their capital Baghdad until its sack by the Mongols in 1258. They were great builders, responsible for such monuments as the Tarik Khana Mosque in Damghan (*left*), the oldest in Iran. Abbasid rule reached a peak in the 8th century under Harun al-Rashid, the caliph of *The Arabian Nights*.

✕ **750** The Abbasids win a decisive victory at the Battle of the Zab (near Mosul in present-day Iraq). They overthrow the last Umayyad caliph, Marwan II, and massacre almost the entire Umayyad family.

✕ **705** Arab armies extend Islamic rule into Central Asia (Bukhara, Samarkand, and Ferghana), the Indus Valley, and part of the Punjab in northwest India (–715).

🌊 **c.740** Nagabhak I, a ruler of the Gurjara–Pratihara Dynasty, unites much of north India and stems the Arab advance into northwest India.

⊕ **c.725** Chinese potters produce the first true porcelain ware at about this time.

⊕ **738** Schools are established in every prefecture and district of China by imperial edict.

⊕ **c.750** The Chinese develop woodblock printing on paper; at first it is used mainly to print devotional Buddhist pictures and literature.

AMERICAS

EUROPE

AFRICA

WESTERN ASIA

SOUTH & CENTRAL ASIA

EAST ASIA & OCEANIA

700–750 A.D.

THE RISE OF JAPAN

CLAIMING DESCENT FROM THE SUN GODDESS Amaterasu herself, the emperors of Japan traced their political origins back to the Yamato rulers who, from a base on the Yamato Plain near the present-day city of Osaka, had brought southern Japan under their rule by about 600 A.D. Chinese culture was at first an important influence, but Japan rapidly developed a rich court culture of its own in which belief in Japan's traditional gods, or kami, lived side by side with Buddhism.

▲ The arrival of Buddhism in Japan in the 6th century stimulated new forms of architecture. Pagodas like this 7th-century example from the Horyuji Monastery in the imperial capital of Nara were built to house relics of the Buddha.

▶ The largest of Japan's keyhole tombs is preserved in a park in the modern city of Sakai. It was built to house the body of the Emperor Nintoku, a 5th-century ruler. This colossal monument is 1,600 feet (500 m) long and is surrounded by three moats.

The earliest history of Japan, the *Nihon Shoki* ("Chronicles of Japan"), was written in the 8th century. It describes the mythological origins of the country and throws little historical light on the origins of the first Yamato kings. Archaeology tells us more. Before 300 A.D. people living around the Inland Sea of southern Japan began to build massive, keyhole-shaped tombs, called *kofun* in Japanese, containing quantities of pottery, weapons, jewelry, and ritual objects such as bronze bells. The tombs probably belonged to high-status warrior chiefs who were rivals for regional power.

By the 4th century the strongest of these local chiefs appear to have been the rulers of the Yamato Plain on Honshu, the largest of the islands that make up Japan. The biggest of the *kofun* tombs, traditionally said to belong to Nintoku, one of the early emperors mentioned in the *Nihon Shoki*, probably dates from the early 5th century. By the end of the 6th century the Yamato kings had extended their rule over southern Japan and for a time may even have controlled an area of southern Korea.

By now a new cultural force—Buddhism—had spread to Japan from Korea and China. With it came other aspects of Chinese culture, including Chinese script and the Chinese calendar. In 710 a permanent imperial court was established at Heijo (modern Nara). It was laid out in a grid-shaped pattern similar

c.300–400 Yamato rule spreads across the central Japanese island of Honshu.

552 Buddhism is introduced to Japan from Korea.

593 Prince Shotoku becomes regent for the Empress Suiko.

604 Prince Shotoku issues the Seventeen Article Constitution.

607 The Horyuji Monastery is founded in Nara.

646 All land in Japan comes under imperial control.

708 The earliest official coinage is introduced in Japan.

710 Heijo (Nara) becomes the new capital of the Yamato emperors.

720 The *Nihon Shoki*, the earliest history of Japan, is written.

794 Emperor Kammu establishes the imperial court at Heian (Kyoto).

894 The emperor breaks off direct contact with China, although Japanese art, architecture, and literature continue to be influenced by China.

1010 The *Tale of Genji*, which many scholars claim to be the world's first novel, is written at the Heian court by Lady Murasaki Shikibu.

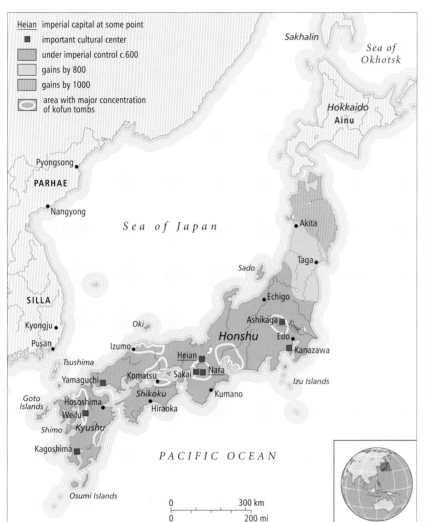

Heian imperial capital at some point
■ important cultural center
   under imperial control c.600
   gains by 800
   gains by 1000
   area with major concentration
   of kofun tombs

Prince Shotoku

One of the first Yamato rulers to emerge from the shadows of prehistory is Prince Shotoku (572–622), seen at right as an infant. Shotoku is supposed to have introduced the "Seventeen Article Constitution," or plan of government, which stressed Chinese principles of loyalty, harmony, and dedication as ideals to be followed in political life. He introduced new ranks of nobility (the twelve "cap ranks"), also based on Chinese practice, which had the effect of weakening the power of the old clan chieftains and promoting men of talent to government office. The constitution gave special protection to Buddhism, and Shotoku is credited with founding many Buddhist temples, including the Horyuji Temple at Nara, which is the oldest surviving monastery compound in Japan. He was so revered as a statesman, sage, and patron of Buddhism that a cult in his honor sprang up shortly after his death.

▲ Imperial power in Japan spread northward up the main island of Honshu from a heartland in the south where the country's successive capitals, Nara and Heian, both lay.

▼ Todaiji Monastery was built in the imperial capital of Nara in 743. Its Great Buddha Hall, shown here, contains the largest statue of the Buddha in Japan, a massive 50 feet (15 m) tall.

to that of Chinese cities. Several important Buddhist monasteries were built nearby.

In time the monks gained so much influence that they began to undermine imperial authority, and in 794 the Emperor Kammu moved the capital to Heian in order to lessen their interference. Heian (today's Kyoto) became the center of a leisured aristocratic culture in which court life itself became a kind of art. Fine handwriting and the composition of poetry were valued above the skills of the warrior, and elaborate rituals of dress and etiquette set the court elite apart from the common people.

750–800 A.D.

AMERICAS

 c.760 Warfare appears to be on the increase among the Mayan cities of the Petén lowlands; some begin to build defensive walls.

 c.790 Murals painted at Bonampak are left unfinished.

c.800 The lowland Maya suffer a sudden decrease in population, which declines from a peak of around 8–10 million people; many cities are abandoned.

c.800 The Toltecs begin to migrate into the Valley of Mexico from the north.

EUROPE

751 Pepin the Short, mayor of the palace, deposes the Merovingian king of the Franks, Childeric III, and becomes king himself.

755 The Byzantine Empire fights a series of campaigns against the Bulgars in the Balkans, forcing them to sue for peace (–764).

756 Abd ar-Rahman, a member of the Umayyad family, founds an independent emirate (Muslim state) at Córdoba in Spain.

778 The Frankish knight Roland and 12 companions are killed in battle at Roncesvalles in the Pyrenees; his death will be celebrated in an epic romance, *The Song of Roland*, written in the 11th century.

787 The Byzantine Empire abandons iconoclasm and orders the worship of images at the Council of Nicaea, a notable victory for the church party over the court.

Mosaic portrait of the Byzantine Empress Irene.

AFRICA

c.750 Arab merchants from North Africa trade across the Sahara, exchanging salt, glass, and horses for African gold, ivory, and slaves.

750 The caliphs of the Abbasid Dynasty take control of Egypt in the wake of their victory over their Umayyad rivals.

c.770 The Soninke Dynasty is established in the Kingdom of Ghana by the ruler of that name, replacing an earlier Berber line.

WESTERN ASIA

c.750 The first paper mill is established in the Islamic empire.

c.760 The Arabs adopt Indian numerals; they are the "Arabic" numerals in general use today.

762 The Abbasid Caliph Al-Mansur establishes a new capital at Baghdad in Iraq.

SOUTH & CENTRAL ASIA

751 The ruler of Tashkent (present-day Uzbekistan) asks the Arabs for protection from the Chinese; an Arab army scores a notable victory over Chinese forces at the Battle of the Talas River.

Rock-cut architecture in India was originally associated with Buddhism and Jainism, but in the 7th and 8th centuries Hindu rulers also commissioned finely carved sanctuaries. The complex at Ellora in central India has monuments from all three traditions, most notably the Hindu Kailasa Temple (*left*).

EAST ASIA & OCEANIA

755 In China the general An Lushan leads a damaging rebellion against the Tang emperors (–763).

763 Tibetan forces sack Chang'an, the western capital of the Tang Dynasty.

780 A power struggle between the monarchy and the nobles weakens the Kingdom of Silla in Korea.

AMERICAS

The extraordinary Mayan murals at Bonampak—"Painted Walls"—only came to the world's attention in 1946, when local people in the Mexican state of Chiapas directed an American photographer to a previously unrecorded three-room building. Its walls were lined with brilliantly colored paintings of war, sacrifice, and feasting, providing a vivid glimpse of Mayan life as the Classic Period neared its end.

EUROPE

☀ **c.790** Irish monks sail to the Faeroe Islands and Iceland in the North Atlantic.

🏛 **792** The Byzantine Emperor Constantine VI makes his mother Irene coruler.

✕ **793** Vikings sack the monastery on Holy Island in northeast England, their first major raid in Europe.

✕ **795** Viking raiders attack the coast of Ireland.

🏛 **797** Irene becomes the first Byzantine empress after having Constantine VI imprisoned and blinded.

✕ **799** First Viking raids along the coast of France.

🏛 **800** Charlemagne, king of the Franks, is crowned Holy Roman emperor by the pope in Rome on Christmas Day.

AFRICA

🏛 **789** The Idrisid Dynasty, adhering to the Shiite branch of Islam, founds an independent caliphate in Morocco.

🏛 **800** The Aghlabid Dynasty rules in Ifriqiya (present-day Algeria and Tunisia), recognizing the authority of the Abbasid rulers of Baghdad.

🏛 **c.800** Arab merchants found trading towns on the East African coast, including Kilwa Kisiwani (in present-day Tanzania).

WESTERN ASIA

⊕ **c.776** Jabir ibn Hayyan writes a scientific treatise describing such techniques as the refining of metals and glassmaking.

🏛 **786** Harun al-Rashid becomes caliph (until 809); a patron of the arts, he is known to history as the ruler of *The Arabian Nights*.

✕ **791** War breaks out anew between the caliph's forces and the Byzantine Empire in Asia Minor (–809).

SOUTH & CENTRAL ASIA

🏛 **756** Dantidurga of the Rashtrakuta Dynasty overthrows the Chalukya Dynasty, which had dominated central India since the 5th century.

☀ **758** Ruling as Krishnaraja I, Dantidurga commissions the Kailasa rock-cut temple at Ellora, one of the great monuments of Indian medieval art.

☀ **788** Birth of Sankaracharya, the great Hindu philosopher and guru; he will reinterpret the Vedas and found four mathas (monastic centers of learning) in India that still survive today (died c.850).

✕ **791** The Tibetans defeat the Chinese at the Battle of Tingzhou, forcing the Tang emperors to abandon their gains in Central Asia.

EAST ASIA & OCEANIA

📖 **780** The Chinese writer Lu Yu writes *The Classic of Tea*, describing the use of tea.

✕ **781** Japan's Emperor Kammu launches a campaign against the Ainu people of northern Honshu that finally brings these early settlers under imperial sway (–812).

🏛 **794** Emperor Kammu of Japan moves his court to Heian, modern Kyoto.

750–800 A.D.

THE EMPEROR CHARLEMAGNE

THE MOST FAMOUS OF THE CAROLINGIAN RULERS *of the Franks is known to history as Charlemagne, literally "Charles the Great." Charlemagne was the son of the first Carolingian king, Pepin the Short, and the great-grandson of Charles Martel, the leader who halted the Arab advance into Europe. In the course of his reign (768–814) he more than doubled the territory of the Franks.*

Frankish royal residence

Frankish Empire in 768

additions to empire by Charlemagne

frontierlands and other areas under influence of Charlemagne

patrimony of St. Peter

▶ Charlemagne consciously set out to revive the glory of the Roman Empire. This small statue of the emperor is based on a Roman model.

According to Einhard, his biographer, Charlemagne was an outstanding figure who always dressed in the Frankish costume of tunic and leggings. Nearly 6 feet (1.8 m) tall, he had boundless energy and was rarely out of the saddle for long. In the course of more than 50 campaigns he extended the Frankish kingdom in all directions: south of the Alps into Italy; east to Saxony in Germany; westward into Brittany, France; and south across the Pyrenees into northeast Spain.

Charlemagne was a devout Christian. He encouraged missionaries, built numerous monasteries and churches, and gave generous grants of land to the papacy. On Christmas Day in the year 800, when on a visit to Rome (the fifth such journey he had made), Charlemagne attended mass in the Church of St. Peter. As he was kneeling in prayer, Pope Leo III placed a crown on his head, and the congregation acclaimed him as "Caesar" and "Augustus." By this act—which in all probability was carefully staged with Charlemagne's full cooperation—the pope established a Catholic emperor in the west independent of the

◀ By tireless campaigning Charlemagne extended the reach of the Frankish realm in several different directions, particularly to the east and south.

768 Charlemagne succeeds his father Pepin the Short as king of the Franks, ruling with his brother Carloman.

771 On the death of Carloman Charlemagne becomes sole ruler.

774 Charlemagne visits Rome for the first time.

781 The pope crowns Charlemagne's son Pepin as king of Italy.

782 The Anglo-Saxon scholar Alcuin, born in York, takes up residence at the court of Charlemagne.

785 Charlemagne subdues Saxony after a long campaign; he begins the conversion of the Saxons to Christianity.

788 The duke of Bavaria (southern Germany) becomes a vassal of Charlemagne.

799 Rioters force the pope out of Rome; he seeks refuge with Charlemagne until restored by Frankish troops.

800 The pope crowns Charlemagne Holy Roman emperor.

A New Style of Building

One of the strongest surviving links with Charlemagne today is the palace chapel at Aachen, in northwest Germany, where he is buried. It is built in the Romanesque style with round arches, vaulted ceilings, and high, small windows. The interior is decorated with mosaics, including the scene of angels around an altar shown at right. As its name suggests, this style of architecture was based on Roman models and particularly on the buildings of the empire in its late, Byzantine-influenced phase; Charlemagne was one of the first patrons to introduce the style north of the Alps. To ordinary men and women the Romanesque buildings spelled out the message that Charlemagne was the successor of the Caesars and could rightfully claim to have restored the glories of the Roman age. Romanesque remained the principal style of building in Europe until replaced by the soaring pointed arches of Gothic architecture in the 12th century.

Byzantine ruler in Constantinople. Charlemagne's coronation came to be viewed as the inauguration of the Holy Roman Empire, an institution that flourished under his successors. It survived for another 1,000 years until abolished by the French ruler Napoleon in 1806.

When not at war, Charlemagne traveled around his vast territories, setting up court wherever he happened to be. He sent roving emissaries to check on the conduct of local administrators, usually bishops and counts. Although he was probably barely literate himself, Charlemagne employed the leading scholars of the day, such as Alcuin of York, at his court, and was a great collector of manuscripts. For this reason his reign is sometimes described as "the Carolingian renaissance," or revival of learning.

✕ **801** Frankish troops capture Barcelona from the Arabs, marking a significant step in the southward drive into Muslim Spain.

🏛 **812** The Byzantine Emperor Michael I recognizes Charlemagne's title in the west.

🏛 **814** Charlemagne dies and is succeeded by his sole surviving son, Louis the Pious.

🏛 **843** Breakup of the Carolingian Empire; Charlemagne's heirs divide it among themselves into three parts at the Treaty of Verdun.

AMERICAS

⊛ **c.800** People in the Eastern Woodlands region of North America begin to farm new varieties of corn and beans, improving food supplies and sparking population growth.

♛ **c.800** In the Peruvian Andes the city of Huari, which at one time had as many as 70,000 inhabitants, is abandoned for unknown reasons, marking the end of the Huari Empire.

⊛ **c.800** The Anasazi are by now establishing villages of adobe houses at cliff sites in the American Southwest.

EUROPE

📖 **810** Death of Nennius, Welsh historian whose *History of the Britons* contains the first reference to King Arthur, described as a Celtic leader.

⚔ **811** Krum, ruler of the Bulgars, defeats Byzantium's Emperor Nicephorus.

♛ **814** On Charlemagne's death his empire passes to his eldest surviving son, Louis the Pious.

♛ **817** Louis divides the empire between his sons, who agree to rule as coregents during his lifetime.

♛ **817** The Bulgars conclude a 30-year peace with the Byzantines.

⚔ **825** Arabs expelled from Spain conquer Crete.

✳ **c.831** A Christian bishopric is established in Hamburg as a center for missionary work in the Viking lands.

♛ **833** Mojmir founds the Kingdom of Moravia.

♛ **835** Viking raiders (mostly Norwegians) start to settle in Ireland.

AFRICA

♛ **c.800** The Kingdom of Kanem is established by the Zaghawa people on the northeastern shore of Lake Chad.

♛ **c.800** The state of Takrur is founded in what is now Senegal, on the western edges of the Kingdom of Ghana.

♛ **809** The city of Fez is founded by the Idrisid caliphs of the Maghreb (Morocco) as their capital city.

WESTERN ASIA

♛ **809** Caliph Harun al-Rashid dies while suppressing a rebellion in Samarkand.

♛ **813** Al-Mamun ascends the throne in Baghdad. His 20-year reign will be called the most glorious in the history of the caliphate.

📖 **c.820** Al-Mamun establishes the House of Wisdom, an academy that sponsors the translation of important Greek and Indian scientific and philosophical works.

⊛ **827** The *Megale Syntaxis* of the Greek astronomer Claudius Ptolemy is translated into Arabic as the *al-Majisti*, or *Almagest*.

⊛ **c.830** The Arab mathematician Al-Khwarizmi introduces the concept of algebra.

SOUTH & CENTRAL ASIA

✳ **c.800** Construction starts at Borobudur, a major Buddhist site on the island of Java that will eventually comprise more than 70 stupas.

♛ **c.800** The state of Srivijaya reaches the height of its power, dominating the sealanes of eastern Indonesia from its base on Sumatra.

♛ **831** The Dravidian Chandella Dynasty comes to power in north-central India; its principal monument will be the spectacular Hindu temples at Khajuraho.

EAST ASIA & OCEANIA

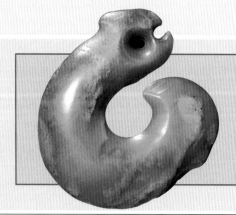

The people who in later times would be known as the Maoris are thought to have arrived in New Zealand in the 9th century. Previously its two main islands were uninhabited, making the new land the last sizable territory to be populated on Earth. Shown at left is a decorative greenstone Maori fish hook.

♛ **c.800** The first Polynesian seafarers, perhaps from the Society Islands, arrive on Aotearoa ("the Land of the Long White Cloud"), later to be known as New Zealand.

✳ **c.800** The populist Amida sect of Buddhism becomes established in the Korean Kingdom of Silla.

AMERICAS

✳ **c.800** First appearance of the Mississippian tradition in eastern America's moundbuilding cultures, typified by large, flat-topped earthworks often referred to as temple mounds.

👑 **820** The Classic Period dynasty at the Mayan city of Copán comes to an end as population levels in the Petén lowlands continue to fall.

EUROPE

✕ **837** Christians and Jews revolt unsuccessfully against Muslim rule in Córdoba, Spain.

👑 **840** Viking settlers in Ireland found Dublin as a trading center.

✕ **840** Louis the Pious dies, and civil war breaks out among his heirs.

✕ **841** Viking raiders invade Normandy.

👑 **843** By the Treaty of Verdun the heirs of Louis the Pious formally break up Charlemagne's empire. Lothair, the eldest, keeps the central territories, Louis the German takes the eastern, and Charles the Bald gets the western Frankish lands.

Britain's semilegendary King Arthur, shown in a medieval tapestry.

AFRICA

✕ **827** The Aghlabid rulers of North Africa conquer Sicily (–878).

☀ **831** The last Coptic Christian armed rising against Egypt's Islamic rulers is put down, leading to a period of rapid conversion to Islam.

✕ **846** An Aghlabid fleet raids Rome.

WESTERN ASIA

👑 **836** Caliph Al-Mutasim transfers the caliphate from Baghdad to Samarra.

✕ **838** Al-Mutasim defeats the Byzantine Emperor Theophilus at the Iris River, but abandons an attempt to take the Byzantine capital Constantinople when a storm destroys his fleet.

✳ **c.840** The Arab astronomer Abu al Fadl Jafar records sunspots.

SOUTH & CENTRAL ASIA

👑 **846** The capital of Sri Lanka is moved south to Polonnaruva to lessen the threat from seaborne Tamil invaders.

👑 **849** The city-state of Pagan is founded in Burma (modern Myanmar).

A temple complex at Khajuraho, India, built by rulers of the Chandella Dynasty.

EAST ASIA & OCEANIA

📖 **801** In China Tu Yu completes the compilation of the *Tung T'ien*—the world's first historical encyclopedia.

👑 **802** Jayavarman II reunites the Khmer people from his base in the Angkor region of Cambodia.

☀ **804** The Tendai and Shingon sects of Buddhism are founded by two Japanese monks, both sent by their emperor on an embassy to China. Both sects will achieve lasting popularity in Japan.

✳ **811** The Tang emperors of China issue "flying cash"—money drafts exchanged by merchants that are an early form of paper currency.

☀ **845** Nonnative religions, including Buddhism and Christianity, are banned in China; Confucianism is restored as the state ideology.

800–850 A.D.

THE MAYA

THE MAYA ORIGINATED IN THE HIGHLANDS OF GUATEMALA. *From about the year 1000 B.C. they began to spread into the lowlands of the Yucatán Peninsula, where they dug canals to drain the swamps to grow food. By the 8th century B.C. they were building monumental temple pyramids, and city-states began to form. Writing, the use of the astronomical calendar, and the sacred ball game were probably adopted from the Olmecs and Zapotecs as long-distance trade developed.*

▲ This life-size stone head was found under the tomb of Pacal, ruler of the city-state of Palenque. It is thought to show him at age 12, when he first came to the throne.

▼ Palenque in the Petén lowlands (see map, p.14) was one of the most powerful Mayan states, reaching a peak during Pacal's 68-year reign in the 7th century.

Around 300 A.D. the Maya living in the Petén lowlands on what is now the Guatemala–Mexico border began to erect stone monuments. These stelae record the deeds of royal ancestors and commemorate important events. Many have survived, hidden in the forest vegetation, and archaeologists have learned how to decipher their inscriptions, which were written in an advanced glyph (picture) script. They paint a scene of more or less continuous conflict between such Mayan city-states as Tikal and Palenque.

Warfare was necessary to supply captives to serve as human sacrifices, who were offered to the gods on fixed dates in the astronomical calendar or to mark important events, such as royal funerals. Victims had their hearts cut out and put on display. Special temple complexes and pyramids were built to provide a setting for these rituals. A corps of priests oversaw and controlled the ceremonies.

Mayan kings were themselves expected to participate in painful rituals involving bloodletting. Typically, their tongues were pierced with cords barbed with thorns. They offered their blood to sustain the gods, who were thought in turn to have undergone ritual sacrifices to sustain the human race.

The Maya used a complex and highly accurate calendar based on precise astronomical observations. In later times they produced sacred books written on bark, which they illustrated with intricate paintings. These works, like their stone carvings, tell us something of their violent cosmos and powerful gods.

Wars and famine brought about by overcultivation of the land may have caused the rapid collapse that led the lowland Mayan cities to be deserted in the years after 800 A.D. The highland settlements survived longer, only to be eventually conquered by Spanish invaders in the 16th century.

👑 **c.750 B.C.** Mayan forms of kingship develop, and the first monuments are built from about this time.

👑 **c.350** The Late Preclassic Period begins with the emergence of the first city-states.

✺ **c.200** The earliest known form of Mayan writing is thought to date from about this time.

The Ballgame

The Maya played a ballgame that was also popular in other cultures across Mesoamerica. In it two opposing teams struck a solid rubber ball around a specially made court. The game seems to have resembled basketball in that the object was to knock the ball through stone rings set high on the court walls. Players were not allowed to touch the ball with their hands, however, only with their hips and knees. They wore protective clothing, including a heavy belt made of wood and leather, and leather hip-pads, kneepads, and gloves. Spectators flocked to the ballcourt to place bets and cheer on their favorite team. The game was not simply a test of strength and skill. For the players it could be, quite literally, a contest to the death. Carvings around the walls of the Great Ballcourt at Chichén Itzá show members of the winning team sacrificing a defeated opponent by cutting off his head, while elsewhere in Mesoamerica the losing captain's heart was sometimes cut out.

▶ The Maya used three basic number symbols: a stylized shell for zero, a dot for one, and a bar for five. Time was recorded in units of 1, 20, 360, 7,200, and 144,000 days. Each interval was represented by a different symbol. The 260-day calender (*right*) had an inner cog with 13 numbers on it rotating around a wheel with 20 named days. As the wheel turned, each number fitted with a day symbol. After 13 days the cycle started anew.

---

c.50 El Mirador, in Guatemala, becomes the largest center of Mayan civilization.

36 The earliest known Mayan calendrical inscriptions, found at Chiapa de Corzo, date from this year.

200 A.D. The eruption of Mt. Ilopango devastates the southern Maya lands. Lake Ilopango now fills the crater left by the eruption.

292 Earliest known lowland inscription, found at Tikal in Guatemala.

c.300 Elaborate monuments are built in the central lowland rainforests, marking the beginning of the Classic Period of Mayan civilization.

c.300 Corbeled arches and vaults first appear in Mayan architecture.

300 Teotihuacán becomes a major influence on the Maya through its trading networks.

c.325 The Maya begin to use stone instead of wood in their buildings.

411 Tikal is the dominant Maya center during the reign of King Stormy Sky.

562 Tikal goes into decline after it is defeated by its eastern neighbor, Caracol.

695 King Jaguar Paw of Calakmul is captured and sacrificed by Ah Cacau of Tikal.

738 Quiriguá becomes the major center of power during the Classic Period.

c.790 Murals painted at Bonampak provide evidence of the warlike character of Mayan civilization.

799 The last monuments are erected at the eastern city of Palenque.

c.800 The "long count" Mayan calendar, with its five separate time cycles, falls into disuse.

c.800 Many central Mayan states fall into decline, marking a shift in power to the highland areas.

c.850 Mayan power and population move north, and Chichén Itzá on the Yucatán Peninsula becomes the dominant Mayan center.

889 The last monuments are erected at Tikal.

AMERICAS

c.850 In the Lambayeque Valley of northern Peru the Sicán art style comes into its own, notably at Batán Grande; distinctive features include black ceramics and shaft tombs.

The Toltecs established an empire in the Valley of Mexico that lasted from the 9th to 12th centuries. Their civilization was a somber one, dominated by concerns with war and sacrifice. This reclining stone figure in Chichén Itzá was shaped to receive the hearts of human victims.

EUROPE

c.850 Magyars from the lands north of the Black Sea settle in Hungary, displacing the Avars.

c.855 Eastern Vikings, known to the Byzantines as Varangians and to the local Slavs as Rus (from which the word "Russia" will derive), establish the state of Kiev in Ukraine.

859 Vikings raid the Mediterranean (–862).

860 Varangians unsuccessfully besiege Constantinople.

862 Saints Cyril and Methodius are sent to convert the Slavs to Christianity.

c.862 Viking Rus under Rurik found the state of Novgorod.

865 Boris I, king of the Bulgars, is baptized into the Orthodox Christian Church.

866 Danish Vikings invade England.

867 Basil I seizes the Byzantine throne from Michael the Drunkard, founding the Macedonian Dynasty, which will oversee a revival in the empire's fortunes.

874 Vikings start to settle Iceland.

878 Oleg becomes ruler of Novgorod; he will unite it and Kiev to form the first Russian state.

AFRICA

c.850 Trade is on the increase in southern Africa, as shown by substantial finds of imported goods at Schroda, a site on the Limpopo River.

862 The Karaouine Mosque is built at Fez.

868 The independent Tulunid Dynasty is established in Egypt (–905).

c.871 Ibn Abd al-Hakam writes the first known history of the Arab conquest of Egypt.

WESTERN ASIA

861 Caliph al-Muttawahil is assassinated by his Turkish bodyguards, now the real power in the Abbasid realm.

869 The Zenj rebellion devastates Mesopotamia (–883).

870 Caliph al-Mutamid temporarily checks the power of the Turkish guards.

873 Muhammad al-Muntazar, twelfth imam of the Shiite Imami sect, disappears; his followers still await his return today.

SOUTH & CENTRAL ASIA

c.850 The Chola State is founded among the Tamil people of southeastern India.

c.850 Uighurs driven westward by Kirghiz and Karluk tribesmen establish a new base in the Tarim Basin region of Central Asia, north of Tibet.

EAST ASIA & OCEANIA

c.850 In China gunpowder is mentioned for the first time.

858 Yoshifusa establishes the Fujiwara family as the power behind Japan's throne, assuming the title of regent.

Low-relief carving from Bakong, Cambodia, dating from Indravarman I's reign.

868 The Diamond Sutra, the earliest known printed book (actually a scroll), is produced in China.

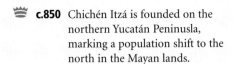
✕ **c.850** The Toltec people establish military supremacy in the Valley of Mexico.

🌊 **c.850** Chichén Itzá is founded on the northern Yucatán Peninusla, marking a population shift to the north in the Mayan lands.

🌊 **862** The long drought afflicting the Mayan lowlands peaks at about this time, contributing to massive population loss in the region.

🌊 **889** The last dated inscriptions found in the Mayan lowlands date from this year.

AMERICAS

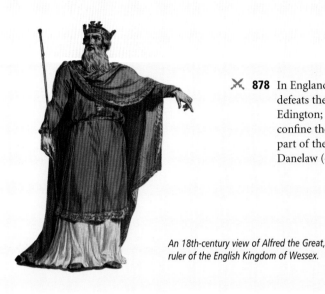

✕ **878** In England Alfred the Great defeats the Danes at the Battle of Edington; he will eventually confine the invaders to the eastern part of the country known as the Danelaw (–886).

🌊 **884** Charles the Fat, ruler of Germany, takes control of the Frankish lands, temporarily reuniting the empire of Charlemagne.

🌊 **888** Charlemagne's empire finally breaks up on the death of Charles the Fat.

An 18th-century view of Alfred the Great, ruler of the English Kingdom of Wessex.

EUROPE

📖 **872** The historian and geographer Al-Yaqubi writes a description of eastern Africa.

⊕ **876** Egypt's Tulunid rulers construct a hospital, racecourse, and the Ibn Tulun Mosque in Cairo (–879).

AFRICA

⊕ **c.890** The Arab astronomer al-Battani calculates the exact length of the year and the precession of the equinoxes.

The Ibn Tulun Mosque in Cairo, made of brick and plaster.

WESTERN ASIA

🌊 **871** Arabs inhabiting what is now southeast Iran and Pakistan establish their independence from the Abbasid caliphs of Baghdad under the Saffarid Dynasty, which goes on to conquer all Iran.

🌊 **c.880** The Palas, a dynasty of Buddhist kings ruling Bengal and Magadha, reach the peak of their power.

🌊 **888** Under Aditya I the Cholas extend their rule up India's southeast coast at the expense of the Pallava rulers to their north.

SOUTH & CENTRAL ASIA

✕ **874** A series of peasant rebellions fatally weakens China's Tang Dynasty, damaging the emperor's authority and strengthening the hand of local warlords (–884).

🌊 **877** Indravarman I ascends the Khmer throne in Cambodia. In his 12-year reign he will extend Khmer rule over the Mon and Thai people to the north and west.

✕ **c.880** Major uprisings weaken the authority of the Korean Kingdom of Silla.

EAST ASIA & OCEANIA

850–900 A.D.

THE VIKINGS

*F*OR THOSE WHOM THEY ATTACKED, THE VIKINGS WERE PIRATES—*robbers who came by sea. Worse still for the Christian monks who chronicled their raids, they were heathens; themselves venerating old Norse gods such as Odin and Thor, they respected neither the church nor churchmen. Viking warriors were indeed fearsome foes, yet there was also a hugely positive side to the Viking achievement. While Norse craftsmen constructed artworks of great beauty, boatborne adventurers settled Iceland and Greenland, made the earliest known European landfall in North America, and helped found the first Russian state.*

▲ Although the Vikings are now best remembered for their fighting skills, they were also fine craftsmen, as this elaborately decorated bronze brooch from Denmark suggests. Viking taste ran to intricate, semiabstract designs in which human and animal heads emerged from a mass of ornamentation.

The Vikings were drawn from a number of different peoples living in the lands we now know as Norway, Sweden, and Denmark. All, however, were linked by a common language, religion, and way of life. Originally farmers for the most part, they were propelled from their Scandinavian homeland apparently by a shortage of available land. Some found previously uninhabited regions to settle, for example, in Iceland and Greenland. Other voyages were carried out for plunder first and only secondarily for settlement.

Different Viking communities tended to concentrate their activities in different areas. Norwegian Vikings began to settle in the islands off the north coast of Scotland at the beginning of the 8th century and then moved down the west coast of Britain and across to Ireland, as well as north to Iceland. Danes attacked the coasts of the western European mainland and, in the mid 9th century, invaded England in force, eventually occupying the eastern half of the country, which they ruled as "the Danelaw." Vikings from Sweden moved across the

Baltic Sea into eastern Europe. Traveling by river, they eventually reached Constantinople, besieging it unsuccessfully in 860. Many of these eastern Vikings settled in the burgeoning river ports as merchants; known to the local Slavs as Rus, they were instrumental in setting up the first Russian state.

By the 9th century the Viking merchant-warriors had built up a large trading network across the Baltic Sea and Europe. The Vikings supplied timber, furs, and honey in exchange for gold, silver, and luxury goods. Slaves were also an important commodity— the very word stems from the Slav peoples whom Viking slavers plundered mercilessly. Another important source of wealth came in the form of protection money, for many western European rulers chose to buy off Viking raiders, offering them huge sums of money in return for guarantees of peace.

⚔ **c.790** Viking raids on western Europe begin.

⚔ **793** Vikings raid Lindisfarne Monastery on Holy Island, off the coast of northern England.

⚔ **c.830** Viking raids on the English and French coast increase, with many towns being sacked.

👑 **c.835** Vikings set up the first winter camps in Ireland.

👑 **845** The Franks buy off Viking raiders by paying the tribute known as Danegeld.

The Viking Longship

The Viking longships represented the most important advance in shipbuilding since the fall of the Roman Empire. First recorded in the late 700s, the slim, beautifully constructed vessels carried warriors on raids across western Europe and into the Mediterranean, and also took settlers in stages across the Atlantic Ocean as far as the North American coast. Like all Viking craft, the longship sailed well; it was narrow and sat shallow in the water, which meant that it could be rowed up rivers. The Vikings sometimes chose to bury their dead leaders in longships, and several of the resulting boat graves have been excavated, providing vital information on the vessels. One famous example was found at Gokstad in Norway in 1880. The Gokstad ship was 75 feet (23 m) long and had 16 oarsmen on each side.

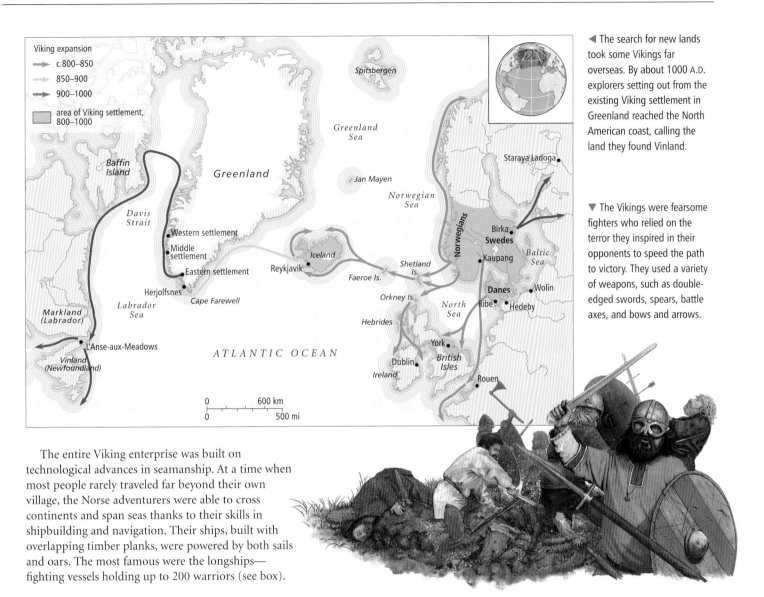

Viking expansion
→ c.800–850
→ 850–900
→ 900–1000
☐ area of Viking settlement, 800–1000

Spitsbergen

Greenland Sea

Baffin Island

Greenland

Jan Mayen

Norwegian Sea

Staraya Ladoga

Davis Strait

Western settlement

Middle settlement

Eastern settlement

Herjolfsnes

Cape Farewell

Labrador Sea

Iceland

Reykjavik

Faeroe Is.

Shetland Is.

Orkney Is.

Hebrides

North Sea

Birka
Swedes
Kaupang
Baltic Sea
Wolin

Danes
Ribe Hedeby

Norwegians

Markland (Labrador)

L'Anse-aux-Meadows

Vinland (Newfoundland)

ATLANTIC OCEAN

York
British Isles
Dublin
Ireland
Rouen

0   600 km
0   500 mi

◄ The search for new lands took some Vikings far overseas. By about 1000 A.D. explorers setting out from the existing Viking settlement in Greenland reached the North American coast, calling the land they found Vinland.

▼ The Vikings were fearsome fighters who relied on the terror they inspired in their opponents to speed the path to victory. They used a variety of weapons, such as double-edged swords, spears, battle axes, and bows and arrows.

The entire Viking enterprise was built on technological advances in seamanship. At a time when most people rarely traveled far beyond their own village, the Norse adventurers were able to cross continents and span seas thanks to their skills in shipbuilding and navigation. Their ships, built with overlapping timber planks, were powered by both sails and oars. The most famous were the longships—fighting vessels holding up to 200 warriors (see box).

✕ **859** Vikings raid ports in Spain and in the western Mediterranean (–862).

〰 **c.860** The first Viking settlement is established in the Faeroe Islands.

✕ **866** The Danish Great Army lands in East Anglia (England).

✕ **867** Danish Vikings occupying England capture the town of York.

✕ **878** Alfred, king of Wessex in southwest England, defeats the Danes at the Battle of Edington.

〰 **882** Oleg makes Kiev capital of the Rus state, which extends from the Gulf of Finland to the Black Sea.

〰 **911** Charles the Simple allows Vikings under Rollo to settle Normandy.

〰 **954** Erik Bloodaxe, the last Viking king of York, is killed at the Battle of Stainmore.

☀ **965** Harald Bluetooth of Denmark becomes the first Scandinavian monarch to be baptized as a Christian.

〰 **c.986** Erik the Red founds Viking settlements in Greenland.

〰 **c.1000** Viking Greenlanders found a shortlived settlement on the North American coast at L'Anse aux Meadows in Newfoundland.

✕ **1013** Danes under Svein Forkbeard invade England.

✕ **1016** Cnut (Canute), Svein's son, is recognized as king of England.

〰 **1028** Cnut unites England, Denmark, and Norway under his rule in a short-lived North Sea empire.

〰 **1035** Magnus the Good is crowned king of Norway.

✕ **1085** A large-scale Danish invasion of England is prepared but is abandoned.

AMERICAS

⊛ **c.900** A remarkable road network is begun in northwestern New Mexico. Radiating out from Chaco Canyon, the roads are up to 35 feet (10 m) wide—far wider than seems necessary for a small society that does not even have pack animals.

⊛ **c.900** The Pueblo Culture of southwest North America begins to build multistory houses arranged around a kiva, a ceremonial center.

♕ **c.900** Mayan civilization finally collapses in the southern lowlands, and the surviving cities are abandoned. Overpopulation, disease, warfare, and social revolution as well as drought are among the theories put forward to explain the collapse.

EUROPE

⊛ **900** A medical school is founded at Salerno on the west coast of southern Italy.

⚔ **c.906** Magyars from Hungary destroy the Slav empire of Moravia and capture Slovakia, which remains a Hungarian possession for the next thousand years.

☀ **910** Duke William of Aquitaine founds the Benedictine Abbey of Cluny, the most magnificent monastery in Europe.

♕ **911** The French king buys off Norman (Northmen) settlers by granting their leader, Rollo, the duchy of Normandy in northern France.

♕ **911** The Byzantine Emperor Leo VI signs a treaty with Oleg, ruler of Kiev, granting Varangian traders from Rus special privileges.

AFRICA

The Fatimid Dynasty took its name from Fatima, daughter of Muhammad and wife of Ali, from whom Shiite Muslims trace the succession of the Prophet. In the course of the 10th century Fatimid rulers established a powerful Shiite state in North Africa that rivaled the Sunni Abbasids for domination of the Islamic world. This Fatimid-era manuscript illustration shows the sport of stick fighting.

WESTERN ASIA

⊛ **c.900** The Persian scholar ar-Razi, known in the west as Rhazes, first classifies matter as animal, vegetable, or mineral. Rhazes also describes infectious diseases.

♕ **c.900** Resurgence of Byzantine power in Anatolia.

♕ **901** Beginning of Saminid rule in Persia.

☀ **935** The text of the Koran, the sacred book of Islam, is finalized.

SOUTH & CENTRAL ASIA

⚔ **c.900** Tribes of Turkish nomads are driven into Afghanistan and Persia by China's westward expansion.

♕ **c.900** The Hindu Shahi family controls the Kabul Valley region in Afghanistan.

♕ **916** The Khitans, horse-riding nomads, found a kingdom in Mongolia.

EAST ASIA & OCEANIA

⊛ **900** Woodblock printing is widely used in China, Japan, and Korea.

♕ **906** Annam, in central Vietnam, achieves independence from China.

♕ **907** The last Tang emperor of China is deposed, and China splits into ten separate states (the Ten Kingdoms).

Chinese woodblock printer at work.

☰ **c.900** The Toltecs establish a capital at Tula (northwest of Mexico City), with a population that grows to about 40,000.

Monumental stone sculptures of warriors from the Toltec capital of Tula.

☰ **929** Abdurrahman III (891–961), emir of Córdoba in Spain, proclaims himself caliph—chief civil and religious leader of the Islamic world.

☰ **930** Norse settlers in Iceland establish the Althing, the world's oldest parliament.

✕ **944** London, England, is beset by a combined force of Danish and Norwegian Vikings.

⊕ **c.945** Gerbert of Aurillac, a French philosopher and future pope, introduces Hindu–Arabic numbers to Europe, but the new system does not at first catch on.

Wood carving from the Igbo Culture, Nigeria.

☰ **909** The Fatimid Dynasty, leaders of the Ismaeli branch of Shia Islam, is established in Kairouan, Tunisia.

✕ **915** The Fatimids invade Egypt.

☰ **935** Algiers founded by Arabs.

⊕ **c.950** The Igbo people of the east Niger Delta (Nigeria) develop an advanced Iron Age culture. They also import copper for bronzemaking, exporting ivory and slaves in return.

📖 **939** Birth of Firdausi, Persian poet (d.1020), who in later life wrote the Persian national epic, the *Shahnama* (Book of Kings).

☰ **945** The Buyids, an Islamic military group, establish themselves in Baghdad, ruling in the name of the Abbasids.

☀ **c.930** A royal inscription recording the foundation of a temple to the god Siva is the first known specimen of the Telugu language of southern India.

✕ **947** The Khitans overrun northeast China and establish the Liao Dynasty, with its capital at Beijing. The Khitans adopt many Chinese administrative techniques.

☰ **935** Koryo, the northern state that gave Korea its name, becomes the dominant power and unifies the country.

☰ **939** Annam (northern Vietnam) wins independence, although nominally remaining a tributary of China.

✕ **939** Revolts against imperial rule set off a period of civil war in Japan.

⊕ **c.945** The Dunhuang star map is produced in China; it uses a type of projection not known in the West until reinvented in 1568 by the Flemish geographer and mapmaker Gerardus Mercator.

AMERICAS

EUROPE

AFRICA

WESTERN ASIA

SOUTH & CENTRAL ASIA

EAST ASIA & OCEANIA

900–950 A.D.

SETTLING OCEANIA

▲ A traditional Maori good-luck charm, this *tiki* is made of jade. New Zealand was the last major landfall of the Polynesians who settled the South Pacific islands in the 1st millennium A.D.

HUNDREDS OF YEARS BEFORE *western peoples crossed the Pacific, Polynesians voyaging in canoes built with stone and coral tools settled islands scattered over an ocean area of 10 million square miles (26 million sq. km). It is impossible to date or track these journeys accurately, but the main migrations took place during the 1st millennium* A.D.—*a period of climate warming, when reliable trade winds and stable seas allowed for long sea journeys. The available evidence suggests that colonization involved deliberate voyaging by seafarers who were able to navigate with remarkable precision.*

Similarities between the languages of Polynesia and Southeast Asia are the strongest evidence that settlers entered the Pacific from the northwest, perhaps as long as 3,500 years ago. Traveling in outrigger canoes, the migrants brought with them a distinctive pottery, staple crops including the banana, breadfruit, and coconut, and domesticated chickens, dogs, and pigs.

By 1000 B.C. the newcomers had settled Fiji, Tonga, and Samoa. In the course of time the skill of potterymaking was lost on the islands, probably for lack of suitable clay; the settlers used shells and gourds instead. A Polynesian farming and fishing culture evolved, with its own distinctive toolkit of shell, coral, and stone implements. From the Tonga–Samoa region Polynesian culture reached the Marquesas Islands by 300 B.C. This island group is ideally placed for dispersal, since it is located at the center of the "Polynesian triangle," with its corners at Easter Island, Hawaii, and New Zealand.

Easter Island was the first of this trio to be settled, by about 300 A.D. On the then densely wooded island the colonists in time established an impressive and enigmatic culture, sculpting huge stone statues and developing the only written language to be found in Oceania. About a century later, seafarers completed the 2,400-mile (3,800-km) voyage to the Hawaiian

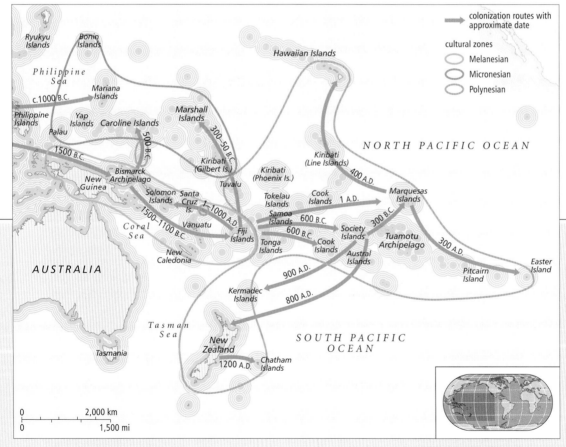

◀ It took many centuries to discover and settle the Pacific islands, but by 1000 A.D. the quest was almost over. The Marquesas Islands were important staging posts in the final round of exploration, serving as a base for voyagers traveling north to Hawaii, east to Easter Island, and south to New Zealand.

Islands, a chain of lush volcanic islands ringed by coral reefs teeming with fish.

When Polynesians reached New Zealand around 800 A.D., they found a very different world. There were no coral reefs, and the climate was too cool to grow the usual crops. Instead, the settlers' staple became the sweet potato, which they supplemented with native plants, including a giant rhizome (root) that needed several days' cooking to make it edible.

Pigs and chickens had not survived the sea voyage, but settlers found other sources of meat. New Zealand's long isolation and the scarcity of natural predators meant that some of its birds had lost the power of flight. The most remarkable were the islands' 19 species of moa, the largest of which stood 12 feet (3.5 m) high. At first the moa were so numerous that the settlers ate only their legs, discarding the rest of the carcass; in time so many were killed that the birds became extinct.

The colonists established tribes, each named for the giant canoe that brought them (they did not call themselves Maoris until after contact with Europeans). By the 13th century they still lived in small, scattered communities; but as the population increased, competition for diminishing food resources produced a militaristic society living in fortresses.

▲ The breadfruit was one of the staple foods that settlers helped spread across Polynesia. Its pulpy fruit is usually roasted or dried and ground into flour.

▼ Statues line a platform on Easter Island. Scholars still argue over the exact meaning of the sculptures, which are thought to represent the spirits of dead ancestors.

Way Finding

In the past it was often claimed that Polynesian seafarers made their discoveries by accident in the course of so-called "drift voyages." Now, however, computer modeling of ocean currents and experiments with replica canoes (*above*) have suggested this explanation is almost certainly wrong. Some scholars now think that the voyagers may have had a deliberate strategy to increase their chances of survival. They believe that they waited for a shift in the normal wind direction (from east to west), then sailed east hoping to find land. If they failed, the homeward journey was thereby made easier when the wind shifted back to its normal direction. The mariners navigated by interpreting natural signs, following birds that roosted on land and looking for the characteristic clouds that form over islands. They also noted telltale changes in wave patterns. At night they studied the heavens, steering toward a point on the horizon where known stars rose in succession.

🏛 **c.0 A.D.** Polynesians begin to spread out from the Marquesas Islands.

🏛 **c.300** Settlers reach Easter Island.

🏛 **318** Earliest date given by carbon dating of a grave on Easter Island.

🏛 **c.400** Settlers from the Marquesas Islands reach Hawaii.

📖 **c.700** The inhabitants of Easter Island begin carving stone statues (called *moai*) set on platforms (*ahu*).

🏛 **800** Destruction of the forests on Easter Island is already under way— an ecological disaster confirmed by pollen records.

🏛 **c.800** Polynesian settlers, possibly from Tahiti or the Society Islands, reach New Zealand's North Island, which they call Aotearoa, "the Land of the Long White Cloud."

🏛 **c.1000** Migrants from Tahiti reach Hawaii and enslave the earlier settlers.

🏛 **c.1250** The global climate begins to deteriorate, making lengthy sea journeys more hazardous. By the time European explorers reach the Pacific, the Polynesians no longer make voyages between the central islands and Easter Island, Hawaii, or New Zealand.

950–1000 A.D.

AMERICAS

c.987 The Toltec ruler Topiltzin is driven into exile in "Tlapallan"— probably the Yucatán Peninsula.

c.1000 Under Toltec influence the Mayan city of Chichén Itzá embarks on two centuries of prosperity.

c.1000 The Chimú people of coastal Peru build a capital, Chan Chan, that at its height will house around 50,000 people.

EUROPE

The origin of the Holy Roman Empire, which came to dominate much of central Europe in medieval times, is usually traced back to the coronation of Charlemagne by Pope Leo III in Rome in 800 A.D. When Charlemagne's empire was divided after his death, the line of succession passed to the rulers of its central lands, incorporating much of modern Germany and northern Italy. The title implied a close relationship between the rulers of this huge realm and the popes, who saw the emperors as their secular champions. Something of the pomp associated with the emperors can be seen in this jeweled golden crown, created for the coronation of Otto I in Rome in 962.

954 Eric Bloodaxe, the last Viking king of York, is killed; England is united under the Anglo-Saxon King Edred.

955 Otto I (912–973), king of the Germans, defeats the Magyars at the Battle of Lechfeld, putting an end to 60 years of Magyar attacks.

962 After conquering Italy, Otto I is crowned Holy Roman emperor in Rome.

966 Six years after founding the Polish state, King Mieszko converts to Roman Catholic Christianity.

AFRICA

965 Birth of al-Hazen, Arab scientist (died 1038) who did pioneering work on vision. His *Book of Optics* remains the most authoritative treatment of optics for centuries.

969 The Fatimids conquer Egypt and found Cairo.

972 A university is founded at Cairo.

c.980 Arab settlers found towns along the eastern coast of Africa.

c.985 By now Islam is penetrating the Christian kingdoms of Nubia.

WESTERN ASIA

963 In Baghdad the Arab astronomer al-Sufi produces *The Book of Fixed Stars*, which mentions nebulae— clouds of interstellar gas and dust.

965 Sviatoslav, ruler of Kiev, crushes the Khazars, a Turkish people who converted to Judaism and built an empire north of the Black Sea.

973 Birth of al-Biruni, Arab mathematician and traveler whose *History of India* helps spread knowledge of Indian numerals.

SOUTH & CENTRAL ASIA

962 Alptigin, a Turkish warrior, founds a Turkic Islamic kingdom in Afghanistan, with its capital at Ghazni. The Ghaznavid Dynasty will control this region for two hundred years.

980 Avicenna (ibn Sina), the great Arab philosopher and physician, is born near Bukhara, in present-day Uzbekistan.

985 Rajaraja inherits the Chola throne in Southeast India. He restores Chola power and goes on to conquer south India.

998 Mahmud of Ghazni, grandson of Alptigin, inherits the Ghaznavid crown, vowing to carry Islamic power into Hindu India.

EAST ASIA & OCEANIA

960 Taizu becomes first emperor of the Song Dynasty.

965 Taizu begins a program of Chinese reunification by taking Szechwan.

976 Chang Ssu-Hsun invents the chain drive for use in a mechanical clock.

978 Chinese scholars begin compiling a 1,000-volume encyclopedia.

979 The Song Dynasty's second emperor takes Wuh-Teh, last of the Ten Kingdoms, completing Chinese reunification.

✳ **c.1000** Leif Eriksson, son of Erik the Red, establishes a settlement in Vinland on the coast of Newfoundland.

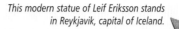
This modern statue of Leif Eriksson stands in Reykjavik, capital of Iceland.

〰 **c.982** Vikings, led by Eric the Red, set up a camp on Greenland, establishing a larger colony four years later.

✕ **982** The Slavs revolt against German rule and recover most of their territories to the east of the Elbe River (–983).

〰 **987** Hugh Capet is crowned king of France, founding the Capetian Dynasty.

☀ **988** Vladimir, ruler of Kiev, marries Anna, sister of the Byzantine Emperor Basil II, and introduces the Eastern Orthodox form of Christianity to his Russian subjects.

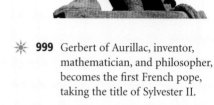

✳ **999** Gerbert of Aurillac, inventor, mathematician, and philosopher, becomes the first French pope, taking the title of Sylvester II.

☀ **1000** The Magyars of Hungary convert to Roman Catholic Christianity.

☀ **1000** King Olaf introduces Christianity to Sweden.

The remains of the Viking settlement at Brattahild in southwestern Greenland.

✳ **c.1000** First Iron Age settlements in Zimbabwe.

〰 **c.1000** The Kingdom of Ghana in today's Mauretania is at the height of its power. It controls the salt and gold trade to Egypt and coastal West Africa.

✳ **977** A hospital is founded in Baghdad that employs 24 physicians and houses a surgery and a department for eye disorders.

✳ **984** Ahmad and Mahmud, two brothers from Isfahan (Persia), make the earliest surviving dated astrolabe.

✕ **1000** Rajaraja invades Ceylon (Sri Lanka) and destroys its capital, Anuradhapura.

Ibn Sina, shown here in a manuscript illumination (seated in red), became the best known of all medieval Arab scholars in the west under the Anglicized version of his name, Avicenna. His *Canon of Medicine*, drawing on the classical writings of Aristotle and Galen, was the most influential medical textbook of the Middle Ages.

✳ **984** Chiao Wei-Yo invents the canal lock—an enclosure with gates at each end—for raising or lowering boats as they pass from one level to another.

〰 **995** Fujiwara Michinaga (died 1027) becomes the true ruler of Japan. Through strategic marriages he becomes the father-in-law to three emperors, a retired emperor, and a crown prince.

✳ **c.1000** By this time the Chinese are burning coal for fuel.

AMERICAS

EUROPE

AFRICA

WESTERN ASIA

SOUTH & CENTRAL ASIA

EAST ASIA & OCEANIA

950–1000 A.D.

THE BIRTH OF RUSSIA

IN 860 A FLEET OF SWEDISH VIKINGS known to the Byzantines as "Varangians" attacked Constantinople. The Varangians had made themselves overlords of Slav tribes living in the forested upper reaches of rivers between the Baltic and Black Seas. Over the next century the Varangians intermarried with the Slavs and created a pagan trading state called Rus, with centers at Novgorod and Kiev. Its chief trading partner was Byzantium, and it was from Byzantium that it received the Christian faith—one of the most significant events in the history of a future great power, Russia.

▲ When Russia converted to Christianity in 988, its rulers chose to adopt the Orthodox form of the faith practiced in the Byzantine Empire.

▶ An illustration from a medieval chronicle shows Vladimir, prince of Kiev, being baptized into the Christian Church. This momentous event helped shape Russian history for centuries to come.

Russian history traditionally begins in 862, with the founding of Novgorod by a Swedish Viking called Rurik. But the origins of the state are older than that. When the Varangians first began exploring the waterways that led from the Baltic to Byzantium, the area was already settled by Slav immigrants from the east. The Varangians quickly came to dominate the territory and captured the market in goods shipped to Constantinople. As well as forest products—furs, timber, and honey—the shipments included captured Slavs; the word "slave" derives from "Slav."

According to a Russian chronicle, the Slavs drove out the Varangians in the mid-9th century, but then fell into such disunity that they begged the Vikings to return as rulers. This was the event that led Rurik to found Novgorod, south of present-day St. Petersburg. Twenty years later Rurik's successor, Oleg, took

Kiev and made it the capital of a more southerly kingdom called "the land of Rus."

Oleg's most famous achievement was an assault on Constantinople with a fleet of 2,000 ships, some of which he allegedly brought ashore and moved on wheels to outflank the

☙ **c.500** East Slavs migrate into the forested region along the river system linking the Baltic Sea in the north with the Black Sea to the south. They displace or absorb Lithuanian and Finnish settlers.	☙ **c.862** The Varangian leader Rurik establishes a capital at Novgorod.	☀ **c.955** Olga, Igor's widow and regent, is baptized into the Orthodox Christian Church.
☙ **c.800** Attracted by the riches of Byzantium and the Islamic world, Swedish Vikings known as Varangians begin to thrust south through the East Slavic heartlands, traveling down the Volkhov and Dnieper rivers to the Black Sea.	☙ **882** Oleg, Rurik's successor, seizes control of Kiev (in present-day Ukraine) and makes it the capital of a domain described in 945 as the "land of Rus."	☙ **962** Sviatoslav, Olga's son, becomes prince of Kiev.
☙ **c.845** Varangians navigate the Volga River, cross the Black Sea, and travel overland to Baghdad.	✕ **907** Oleg launches a large-scale attack on Constantinople, forcing the Byzantines to sue for peace.	✕ **965** Prince Sviatoslav conquers the Khazars who occupy the steppes north of the Black Sea. But Russian control of the steppes is soon lost to the Pechenegs, nomad raiders who prey on traders following the river route from Rus to Byzantium.
✕ **860** Varangians mount their first attack on Constantinople.	☙ **911** Oleg returns to Rus with a trade treaty under which Byzantium is obliged to pay for the upkeep of Russian traders in Constantinople.	✕ **971** The Byzantine Emperor John Tzimisces defeats Sviatoslav's army and forces him to give up all the land he has won. On his homeward journey Sviatoslav is murdered by Pechenegs.
	✕ **943** Igor, Oleg's successor, invades Azerbaijan.	

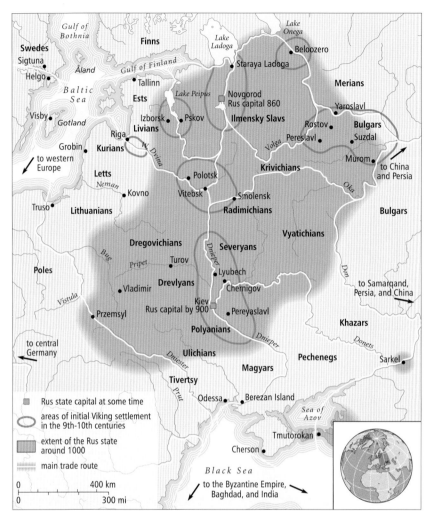

city's defenses. Whatever the truth of the story, Oleg certainly succeeded in winning favorable trading privileges from the Byzantines.

Trade with Byzantium brought the pagan Varangians into contact with Christianity. The first royal convert was Olga, widow of a Kievan prince and mother of Sviatoslav, the first prince of Kiev to bear a Slav name. Sviatoslav clung to the old Norse gods, and his militant paganism was at first shared by his son Vladimir. Yet in 988, 11 years after gaining the crown, Vladimir ordered the wholesale conversion of his people to Christianity.

Legend says that he chose the Orthodox faith after a commission reported on the merits of the different religions and churches. The men dispatched to Constantinople described in ecstatic terms how, inside the church of St. Sophia, they did not know if they "were on heaven or on earth." In fact, Vladimir's reasons for embracing Orthodox Christianity were political as much as spiritual: His reward for converting was an alliance with Byzantium through marriage to the emperor's sister.

Vladimir's decision had immense consequences. If Russia had converted to Islam, world history would have been incalculably different. At the same time, by embracing the Eastern Orthodox faith rather than Roman Catholicism, Russia was bound to develop along different lines than the rest of Europe.

◄ The Viking presence in Russia developed along the major rivers, which were used to trade southward to the Black Sea. In time the separate settlements joined together into the kingdoms of Novgorod and Kiev.

977 Vladimir, a son of Sviatoslav, wins a war of succession with his two brothers and becomes the new ruler of Rus. According to a chronicler, he is a militant pagan who even encourages human sacrifice to the gods.

988 Vladimir converts to Orthodox Christianity and orders his people to be baptized en masse on the banks of the Dnieper River. In return he is given the hand of the Byzantine emperor's sister, Anna.

989 As part of the settlement between Russia and Byzantium, Vladimir sends 6,000 Russian troops to Constantinople. The troops become famous as the Varangian Guard, the emperor's elite military unit.

Wood and Silver

Medieval Novgorod was built entirely of wood. Its people lived in wooden houses, used wooden drains, worshiped in wooden churches, walked on streets surfaced with split pine logs, and wrote on birch bark or boards (*right*). Russian archaeologists have uncovered more than 1,000 buildings preserved in the waterlogged ground. Dendrochronology, the science of tree-ring dating, has revealed that the oldest surviving wooden street was laid out around 953; up to 25 different layers of paving have been found in some thoroughfares. The excavations also turned up many coin hoards, as the Varangians traded their furs and other goods for silver dirhams minted in Central Asia. The dirham, which was the standard currency in Eastern Europe, became a Viking status symbol: A 10th-century Arab writer records that a Varangian woman was entitled to wear one silver necklace for every 10,000 dirhams (about 64 lb/29 kg of silver) her husband possessed.

FACTS AT A GLANCE

Abbasid Dynasty
The dynasty of caliphs that controlled most of the Islamic world from 750 to 1258 from their capital at Baghdad, Iraq. They claimed descent from Abbas, the uncle of Muhammad.

adobe
Mud mixed with straw for extra bonding strength then dried in the sun for use as a building material.

Aghlabid Dynasty
A Muslim Arab dynasty that ruled much of North Africa from 800 to 909. They were based in present-day Tunisia and Algeria, and at one time their control extended to Sicily and southern Italy.

Almagest
The most influential work on astronomy of the Middle Ages. Written in Greek by the Egyptian astronomer Ptolemy (c.90–168 A.D.), it was translated into Arabic as *Al-Majisti* ("Great Work"). Medieval Latin translations reproduced the title as *Almagesti*.

Althing
The parliament of Iceland (the word is Icelandic for "general assembly"). The oldest parliament in the world, it was established in 930 and met each summer as both legislature and court on the Thingvellir Plain, northeast of Reykjavik.

amber
Fossilized resin from coniferous trees. Ranging in color from pale yellow to deep brown, the substance has been prized from ancient times for its decorative use in jewelry. Some of the best amber is found on the south shore of the Baltic Sea.

Amida sect
Populist Buddhist sect that preached salvation in paradise for all who worshiped a monk named Amitabha who had attained Buddhahood. The cult, which developed in China in the 6th century, spread to Korea and then to Japan, where it formed the basis of the later Pure Land sect.

Anasazi Culture
An agrarian civilization of the American Southwest that, having first emerged as the "Basketmaker Culture" around the 2nd century B.C., reached its apex around 800 A.D. in the adobe-built towns of the Pueblo Period.

Anglo-Saxons
Germanic peoples (Angles, Saxons, and Jutes) who migrated to Britain from Germany and Denmark c.450 A.D. and established a number of kingdoms there. In time the Anglo-Saxons became known as the English.

Annam
A state located in what is now northern Vietnam that was conquered in about 214 B.C. by the Chinese, who named it An-Am, "Peaceful South." Independent from 939, Annam was incorporated into Vietnam in 1946.

Arthur
A legendary British king who may have some basis in reality: Historians think a British war-leader named Arturus may have fought a number of battles against the Anglo-Saxons who invaded Britain in the 6th century A.D. However, there is no mention of Arthur in any contemporary historical record, and the legends of Arthur and the knights of the Round Table were not written down until the 12th century by Geoffrey of Monmouth and other chroniclers.

Avars
Nomads from Central Asia who migrated westward in the 6th century A.D. into the region of Hungary previously occupied by the Huns. They established a khanate (state) on the upper Danube River from which they made frequent raids into the Balkans and central Europe. They were defeated by Charlemagne in 796.

Bantu
A people originating in West Africa who migrated slowly to the south and east between around 200 and 650 A.D., carrying with them the skills of settled agriculture and ironworking and a common language.

barbarian
Term used by the Romans to describe all peoples living outside the frontiers of the Roman Empire, but in particular the Germanic-speaking peoples settled on its northern frontiers.

Benedictine Order
Order of monks and nuns founded by the Italian St. Benedict in the 6th century. Benedictines had a strong influence on learning in medieval Europe.

Berbers
The original inhabitants of North Africa, occupying the area west of Egypt as far as the Atlantic coast. Their lands were colonized by the Phoenicians and the Romans in ancient times, and were invaded by the Arabs in the 7th century A.D. After some resistance they converted to Islam.

Bulgars
Central Asian nomads, the Bulgars joined the westward push of peoples from this region in the 7th century. They ended up in the Balkans, first as invaders and then as mercenary soldiers employed by the Byzantine Empire.

Buyid Dynasty
Also known as the Buwayhid Dynasty. The line of caliphs established after Ahmad ibn Buwayh, a Shiite warlord from the Iranian mountains, seized power in Baghdad, Iraq, in 945.

Byzantium
City founded as a Greek colony on the European side of the Bosphorus on a site now occupied by part of Istanbul. Renamed Constantinople in 330 A.D., it became first the eastern capital of the Roman Empire then sole capital of the Byzantine Empire. The name "Byzantium" is also sometimes applied to the Byzantine Empire itself.

caliph
Derived from the Arabic *khalifah*, or "representative," this title was conferred on those rulers of the Muslim world in whom the authority of the Prophet as Allah's voice on Earth was believed to be perpetuated.

Capetian Dynasty
French dynasty founded by Hugo Capet in 987 that ruled until 1328, when it was succeeded by the House of Valois.

Carolingian Dynasty
The dynasty of Frankish kings descended from Pepin of Landen (died 640 A.D.), who became mayor of the palace to the Merovingian King Chlothar II. His descendants continued to hold the office of mayor of the palace until Pepin the Short (c.714–c.768) deposed the last Merovingian king and made himself ruler of the Franks in 751. The greatest of the Carolingians was Charlemagne, or Charles the Great, who was crowned emperor in 800. The dynasty derives its name from Carolus, the Latin form of Charles.

Carolingian Renaissance
The name given to the revival of learning during Charlemagne's reign. With the fall of the Roman Empire literacy all but disappeared in western Europe for several centuries, except among churchmen. Even kings were unable to read or write; Charlemagne himself could barely sign his name. But he collected manuscripts and encouraged scholars to study the works of Roman philosophers and early church writers.

Carthage
The defeated rival of ancient Rome, Carthage endured a second period of influence after 455 A.D., when it became the capital of the kingdom founded in North Africa by the Vandals.

Chaco Canyon

Important Pueblo Culture center in northwestern New Mexico. The hub of a road network, 10th-century Chaco Canyon had several large buildings, each containing hundreds of rooms.

Chalukya Dynasty

Southern Indian dynasty that ruled in the Deccan region, with interruptions, from 535 to 1200 A.D. The Chalukyas' imperial heyday came in the reign of Pulakesin II (608–42). Their spectacular capital, Badami, was remarkable for its temples, their spires and pinnacles cut directly from the rock.

Champa

With its capital near what is now Da Nang, this Hindu kingdom founded by Indian traders dominated central Vietnam from its foundation in about 200 A.D. right through to the start of the 2nd millennium.

Chandella Dynasty

A line of kings whose capital at Khajuraho, central India, became the focal point of a 300-year golden age that started around 900 A.D., with achievements in literature, philosophy, the arts, and above all architecture.

Chenla

A state that emerged among the Khmer people of Cambodia in about 400 A.D. By about 550 it had united all the Khmer people in a single empire and had grown strong enough to overthrow the neighboring state of Funan, based in the Mekong River Valley. It was at its height around 700 but began to decline shortly afterward.

Chichén Itzá

Spectacular Mayan city in Mexico's Yucatán Peninsula. Founded around the 9th century, it did not reach its peak until the arrival of Toltec exiles from central Mexico at the end of the 10th century.

Chimú Culture

South American civilization that flourished on the coast of Peru from the 11th to the 15th centuries, when it was conquered by the Incas. As well as producing fine work in gold and pottery, the Chimú built aqueducts and possibly developed a system of writing by painting patterns on beans.

Chola Dynasty

Southern Indian dynasty that came to the fore in about 850 A.D., when Vijayalaya seized the city of Tanjore. Their empire extended overseas to include parts of modern Malaysia and Indonesia, but declined from the mid 11th century.

Cholula

Located in central Mexico, Cholula was an important center during Mesoamerica's Classic Period (100–800 A.D.); its Great Pyramid was the largest in Mexico. The exact relationship between Cholula and its larger neighbor, Teotihuacán, is not known, but it appears to have survived longer than Teotihuacán, and some historians believe it may have been responsible for the latter's destruction in about 650.

Colchis

An ancient country on the Black Sea (part of today's Republic of Georgia). According to Greek legend, it was the land of the Golden Fleece sought by Jason and the Argonauts.

Confucianism

The doctrine derived from the teachings of the celebrated Chinese administrator and philosopher Confucius (551–479 B.C.), known in China as Kongfuzi. In later times Confucianism, which emphasized learning, respect, and good conduct, became a state religion in China.

Copts

Members of the Coptic Church, a branch of Christianity founded in Egypt in the 5th century that still survives today. The Copts were Monophysites and were frequently persecuted as heretics.

Danegeld

A tax paid to Viking raiders or occupation forces by peoples eager to avert attacks. In England it was imposed from 991 A.D. by Anglo-Saxon kings to raise the money to pay tribute to the Viking invaders of England.

Danelaw

Area of north and east England granted to Danish Vikings in the 9th century. The Danelaw survived as a separate territory until 954, and its settlers had a lasting influence on local language and culture.

dendrochronology

Analysis of the annual growth of tree rings to date past events. Variations in climate year by year produce distinctive rings. Dating involves comparing samples from archaeological sites with old living trees or with timber used in a structure of a known date. The year when the trees were felled can be determined by locating the point where the rings of the samples match.

Diocletian

246–316 A.D. Roman emperor whose administrative and financial reforms helped restore the fortunes of the Roman Empire.

Dravidians

The original inhabitants of southern India, the Dravidians were marginalized by the expansion of Aryan and later Muslim civilizations from the north.

Eastern Roman Empire

Eastern half of the Roman Empire, with its capital at Constantinople, whose founder, Emperor Constantine, divided the empire at his death in 337 A.D. While the Western Empire collapsed in 476, the Eastern Empire survived to become the Greek-speaking Byzantine Empire.

Ephthalite Huns

Also known as the White Huns. A branch of the Huns who overran much of the Sassanian Empire of Persia in the 4th to 6th centuries A.D. and helped bring about the downfall of the Gupta Dynasty in northern India in about 455.

Fatimid Dynasty

Muslim Shiite dynasty founded in Tunisia in 909 by Ubayd Allah, who claimed descent from the Prophet Muhammad's daughter Fatima and her husband Ali. In 969 the Fatimids conquered Egypt, founding the city of Cairo as their capital. The dynasty survived until 1171.

feudal system

Medieval European social and economic system characterized by the granting of land in return for political and military service to an overlord.

Franks

A Germanic people who settled east of the Rhine River in what is now the Netherlands in the 3rd century B.C. After the fall of the Western Roman Empire the Frankish kings gradually conquered most of Gaul (France), Italy, and Germany, creating an empire that lasted from the 6th to the 9th century. France is named for them.

Frisians

A Germanic people who occupied the coast and offshore islands of a region approximating to the present-day Netherlands and part of north Germany. They were conquered and converted to Christianity by Charlemagne in 784.

Fujiwara
The ruling clan in Japan from 858 to 1185. During that period the office of emperor became merely ceremonial, while real power was exercised by Fujiwara chancellors and regents.

Funan
A trading kingdom in what is now Cambodia and southwestern Vietnam that grew rich on the profits from the seaborne trade between India and China. It was overthrown by Chenla in about 550.

Ghana
Not to be confused with today's west African country, the Kingdom of Ghana was established farther north, in what is now northern Senegal and southern Mauritania. It arose around the year 500 A.D., thriving on the increasingly important trans-Saharan trade.

Ghaznavid Dynasty
Turkish Muslim dynasty founded at Ghazni in Afghanistan in 962. For more than 200 years the Ghaznavids ruled Afghanistan and the neighboring Punjab, where they established a new capital at Lahore in 1160.

glyph
A unit of the symbolic script carved in stone by the Mayans. Glyphs were used to represent both words and numbers.

Greek fire
An inflammable substance used as a weapon by the Byzantines. Its formula (a state secret) has not survived, but it probably involved combinations of naphtha, sulfur, petroleum, bitumen, and other chemicals. Greek fire was used either as a missile hurled from a catapult or as a flamethrower.

Gupta Dynasty
The dynasty founded by Chandragupta I, ruler of Magadha, that came to control an empire in northern India from the 4th to 6th centuries A.D. Hindu culture flourished under the Guptas.

Gurjara Dynasty
Nomads of Central Asian origin who migrated into the Indian subcontinent in the 4th and 5th centuries A.D., the Gurjaras established a ruling dynasty in the region of Rajasthan in northern India in about 550. The Gurjara–Pratihara Dynasty, which united much of north India in the 8th century, may have been descended from them.

hajj
The pilgrimage to Mecca that every Muslim is obliged to undertake, if at all possible, at least once in the course of his or her lifetime.

heathen
A word used by Christians to describe an individual or nation that has not converted to Christianity.

Heian Period
The period of Japanese history from 794 to 1192, beginning with the shifting of the nation's capital from Nara to Heian (modern Kyoto). The era came to be seen as a golden age of peace, prosperity, and national self-confidence during which the country at last broke free from the cultural domination of China.

hijra
Also known as the Hejira. The "migration" of Muhammad and his followers from a hostile Mecca to the city of Medina, 250 miles (400 km) to the north on the Arabian Peninsula. It took place in 622 A.D., which has since been Year 1 in Islamic chronology.

Holy Roman emperor
A title bestowed by the pope from medieval times on a leading central European ruler, thought of as the chief secular champion of the Christian cause. Most Holy Roman emperors were Germans belonging to the Hohenstaufen or Hapsburg Dynasties. The first Holy Roman emperor was the Frankish Emperor Charlemagne, crowned in the year 800; the title was finally abolished by Napoleon Bonaparte in 1806.

housecarl
A member of a Danish or Anglo-Saxon ruler's troop of bodyguards, owing allegiance to the king.

Huari Culture
Culture that flourished in the Andean region of Peru from the 6th to 9th centuries. It centered on the city of Huari in the Ayacucho Valley, which covered almost 2 square miles (5 sq. km) and may have housed 70,000 people.

Huns
Nomadic peoples from Central Asia, one group of whom (known as the Black Huns) migrated to eastern Europe in about 370 A.D. and established a kingdom in present-day Hungary. Legendary for their violence, they disappeared from history after the death of their leader Attila in 453. *See also* Ephthalite Huns.

Iconoclast Controversy
Religious conflict that split the Byzantine Empire in the 8th and 9th centuries, when a succession of emperors sought to forbid the veneration of icons (holy images) on the grounds that it contravened the biblical injunction against the worship of graven images. The iconoclasts (icon destroyers) eventually lost the argument in 843, when icons were restored to imperial favor.

Idrisid Dynasty
An Islamic dynasty that ruled a kingdom in what is now the northern part of Morocco from 789 to 926. The founder of the dynasty was Idris I, who claimed descent from Ali, Muhammad's son-in-law.

Igbo
People of the eastern Niger Delta lands who developed an advanced Iron Age culture centered on Igbo-Ukwu, which was probably a royal site. The Igbo used local iron ores and imported copper to make fine swords and bronze ornaments.

Imami sect
The main division of Shiite Islam, whose imams, or leaders, are held to be descended from the Prophet Muhammad's son-in-law Ali.

Ismaeli sect
Shiite Muslim movement expressing allegiance to Ismael, eldest son of the Sixth Imam, or religious leader, which started as a secret underground splinter group and rose to power in North Africa under the Fatimid Dynasty. The Druse people of modern Lebanon are a breakaway group of the Ismaelites.

Juan-Juan
An alliance of Central Asian nomads that controlled the northern frontier of China from the early 5th to mid 6th century A.D. They included the Avars, who later harassed eastern Europe.

Kanem
Central African state established in about 800 A.D. by nomadic herders who settled down to pursue a more agricultural lifestyle. By the 11th century it had become a major trans-Saharan trading center.

Kharijites
An early Islamic sect that refused to accept the authority of Uthman, the third caliph, and Ali, the fourth caliph. They withdrew to an area of Iraq (*khariji* means "one who goes out"), from where they launched a number of violent uprisings and were responsible for the murder of Ali in 661. They were eventually suppressed by the Abbasids in Iraq, but survived in other parts of the Islamic world, especially North Africa, where they remain today.

Khazars
People of Turkish origin who in the 7th century A.D. established an empire between the Caspian and Black Seas, stretching north to the middle course of the Volga River. Converts to Judaism, the Khazars were a significant factor in preventing Arab expansion to the Caucasus.

Khitans
Horse-riding nomads related to the Mongols who, in the 10th century A.D., established an empire centered on Beijing and administered on semi-Chinese lines.

Khmer Empire
Established in the 6th century A.D. in what are now Cambodia and Laos, the Khmer Empire reached its height in the 10th to 12th centuries, when its capital was Angkor Wat.

kofun
Massive burial mounds found in Japan and dating from about the 4th to the 6th centuries A.D. They are known as "keyhole tombs" for their shape.

Koguryo
The earliest Korean state, founded in the 1st century A.D. and strongly influenced by Chinese culture. Koguryo was conquered by the neighboring state of Silla in 668.

Koran
The holy text of Islam. Believed to have been divinely dictated to the Prophet Muhammad in the form of long poems, or *shuras*, it was brought together in book form in about 650 A.D. by the Caliph Uthman.

Koryo
Kingdom founded in 918 A.D. that unified Korea into almost its present form by the 11th century.

Liang Dynasty
Dynasty ruling southern China from 502 to 557.

Lindisfarne
An island (also known as Holy Island) off the coast of Northumberland, northeast England. The Irish missionary monk Aidan founded a monastery there in the early 7th century, which was destroyed by Viking raiders in 793.

Lombards
A Germanic people who established a kingdom in northern Italy from 568 to 774.

Macedonian Dynasty
Byzantine dynasty founded in 867 by Emperor Basil I. The early Macedonian emperors regained territories lost to Muslim rulers, expanded trade, and fostered a revival of learning. After a period of decline the dynasty ended in 1081.

Maghreb
Also spelled Maghrib. The western part of Islamic North Africa covered by the modern states of Libya, Tunisia, Algeria, Morocco, and Mauritania.

Magyars
People originating in northeastern Europe who gradually migrated south to found the Kingdom of Hungary in the late 9th century.

Makurra
Also spelled Mukurra. The largest of the three states to emerge in Nubia after the collapse of Meroë in 350 A.D. (the other two were Nobatia—conquered by Makurra in the 8th century—and Alwa). Christianity was introduced into Makurra in the 6th century. After the Arab conquests of the 7th century its people came under great pressure to convert to Islam. Makurra was finally conquered by the Arabs in the 14th century.

Mayan long count
In the complex calculations of the Mayan calendar, the reckoning of long periods of time in terms of *baktuns*, each equivalent to 144,000 days (approximately 400 years). History was measured in cycles of 13 baktuns; the current cycle, starting in 3114 B.C., ends in 2012.

Merovingian Dynasty
The dynasty of Frankish kings that ruled the kingdom founded by Clovis from 481 until 751, when they were supplanted by the Carolingians.

Mesopotamia
The ancient Greek name, meaning "between the rivers," for the fertile land between the Tigris and Euphrates rivers in southern Iraq. Here the Sumerians, Babylonians, and Assyrians established their civilizations.

missionary
Someone who undertakes the task of spreading the Christian religion to unconverted peoples.

Mississippian Culture
The successor to the Hopewell Culture, this tradition emerged along the Mississippi Valley in the 9th century: It organized agriculture on an unprecedented scale and constructed large and elaborate flat-topped burial mounds.

Moche Culture
The culture associated with the Moche River valley in coastal northern Peru, which flourished from about the 1st to 8th century A.D. The Moche people built ceremonial centers with platform mounds; one of them, the Pyramid of the Sun, is among the largest in the Americas.

monasticism
An austere way of life followed by groups of men or women living in a religious community. Many religions practice monasticism, including Buddhism and Christianity. Monasticism developed in the early Christian church in the 3rd and 4th centuries.

Monophysite sect
Christians who believed that the person of Jesus Christ remained wholly divine even when he took human form (orthodox teaching holds that Jesus has two natures: human and divine). The Monophysites were condemned at the Council of Chalcedon (451), but the Coptic, Syrian, and Armenian churches retained some aspects of Monophysite belief.

Moravia
An area along the Morava River, a tributary of the Danube, that was settled by Slavs in the 6th century. The Moravians subsequently swore allegiance to the Franks.

Nara
The first imperial capital of Japan, from 710 to 784, and an early center of Japanese Buddhism.

Nestorian sect
A Christian sect that stressed the separateness of Jesus's two natures, human and divine. The doctrine was propounded by the Syrian ecclesiast Nestorius, patriarch of Constantinople from 428 to 431, when he was condemned as a heretic. To escape persecution, many of his followers emigrated to Iraq, Syria, and Persia.

Normans
Descendants of the Norsemen who in the 10th century settled in northern France and adopted French language and culture, while retaining their aggressive Viking energy. The Normans conquered England, Scotland, parts of Wales and Ireland, southern Italy, Sicily, and Malta.

Norse
Adjective applied to all the Scandinavian Vikings—Danes, Swedes, and Norwegians.

Northern Zhou Dynasty
Dynasty that seized power in western Wei (the northernmost kingdom of China) in 557 and expanded its power base into eastern Wei and southwest China. In 581 the Northern Zhou were overthrown by one of their generals, Yang Jian, who reunited China and founded the Sui Dynasty.

Nubia
The region to the south of Egypt on the Nile River, roughly equivalent to modern Sudan.

obsidian
A hard black glass, formed naturally in the course of volcanic eruptions and valued by many early civilizations for use in the manufacture of blades and jewelry.

Olmecs

A people who flourished from about 1250 to 200 B.C. in southern Mexico and neighboring regions and who were responsible for the first great culture of the central American region. Olmec influence lingered on in the Mayan and other cultures for many centuries.

Orthodox church

Also known as the Eastern Orthodox church. The branch of the Christian church recognized throughout the Greek-speaking world of the eastern Mediterranean. Its spiritual head was, and is, the patriarch (archbishop) of Constantinople. The Slavs of eastern Europe and the Russians subsequently became part of the Orthodox church.

Ostrogoths

A Germanic people living in the area north of the Black Sea who were conquered and displaced by the Huns in about 370 A.D. Under their leader Theodoric (c.455–526) they moved into Italy in 488 and established a kingdom that lasted until 555.

outrigger canoe

A canoe given additional stability by long floats attached parallel to the hull.

Paekche

An ancient Korean kingdom. Paekche's fortunes were in decline before victory over Koguryo in 553 appeared to promise a return to greatness. But Paekche's exhausted forces were promptly crushed by the third Korean kingdom, Silla, opening the way for the peninsula's eventual unification.

pagan

A word applied by Christians to nonbelievers who worshiped many gods.

pagoda

A religious monument introduced with Buddhism into China and other Southeast Asian countries. Derived from the Indian stupa—a pinnacled dome housing Buddhist relics—Chinese pagodas are multistoried buildings whose design was based on existing watchtowers.

Pala Dynasty

Founded by Gopala in 750, but brought to prominence by his son Dharmapala (770–810), this dynasty built a formidable empire in Bengal and Bihar, in northern India.

Pallava Dynasty

Southern Indian dynasty that ruled from the 4th to the late 9th century, when their lands were taken over by Chola rulers. Their monuments include the rock-cut temples of Mahabalipuram.

papacy

The ruling body of the Catholic church, headed by the pope (the bishop of Rome). In the Middle Ages the pope was recognized as the undisputed head of the church in the west and also had considerable political power as the ruler of the Papal States. His authority was not, however, recognized in the eastern Christian lands that subscribed to the Orthodox church.

Pechenegs

Turkic nomads who occupied the steppes north of the Black Sea from the 6th to the 12th centuries. A menace to 10th-century Russian traders and a threat to the Byzantine Empire, their forces were finally annihilated outside Constantinople in 1091.

Petén

In historical terms the lowland rainforest region of the Yucatán Peninsula, straddling the present-day Mexico–Guatemala border; now a province of Guatemala.

Polynesians

Seafaring people who probably originated in Southeast Asia and the East Indies, and whose progess was marked by the spread of the Lapita Culture. Notable for their navigational skills and double-hulled dugout canoes, they settled Samoa and Tonga by about 1000 B.C. and spread out across other Pacific islands in the course of the next two millennia.

pre-Columbian

Adjective used to describe objects, cultures, and peoples of the Americas predating the arrival of the explorer Christopher Columbus in 1492.

Pueblo Culture

A culture in southwestern North America characterized by large apartment settlements centered on a ceremonial building called a kiva. The first pueblos were built in about 900 A.D.; by the year 1000 many of them consisted of 200 rooms or more.

Qi Dynasty

Dynasty that ruled southern China from 479 to 502 A.D.

Rashtrakuta Dynasty

Indian dynasty founded by Dantidurga in the 8th century, which overthrew the Chalukya Dynasty to take control of central India.

Roman Catholic

Member of the Western or Latin Christian church, headed by the pope, the bishop of Rome. Today the Roman Catholic church is the largest Christian community, with a membership of about 1 billion.

Romanesque

A style of architecture found throughout western Europe from the 8th to 12th centuries, marked by rounded arches and vaulted ceilings supported on solid piers. Arches, doors, and windows frequently have incised decorations.

Rus

The first Russian state, which was founded by Swedish Vikings in the 9th century centered on the towns of Novgorod and Kiev. The word may derive from the Finnish name for Sweden, *Ruotsi*.

Sassanian Dynasty

Dynasty of Persian kings (224–651 A.D.) named after Sassan, grandfather of Ardashir I, the first Sassanian ruler.

Saxons

Germanic people inhabiting the Baltic coast of north Germany. In the late 8th century they resisted for 32 years Charlemagne's campaigns to absorb them into the Frankish Empire, but were eventually conquered and converted to Christianity in 785. Saxony, their homeland, later became a powerful medieval duchy.

Seljuk Turks

Nomadic fighters from Central Asia, the Seljuks became Muslims on arrival in West Asia around the 10th century. They went on to found an empire, reinvigorating an enfeebled Sunni Islam.

Shiites

Muslims of the Shia-i Ali, the "Party of Ali," claiming allegiance to Muhammad's son-in-law and to those imams believed to be his spiritual successors.

Shingon sect

Form of Buddhism introduced into Japan from China in 806, which lays stress on the sutras (sacred Buddhist texts), mandalas (sacred symbols of the universe), and secret magical phrases. Shingon means "True Word."

Sicán Culture

A civilization that arose in the Peruvian Andes in about the 9th century. Evidence of large-scale irrigated agriculture and sophisticated metalworking have been found at the the city-sized site of Batán Grande.

Silla

A small state in southeast Korea that conquered its neighbors, Paekche and Koguryo, to dominate the Korean peninsula from about 668 to 935. Its capital city, Kyongju, was modeled on Chinese cities, and its rulers were Buddhist.

Slav
Originally from Central Asia, the Slavs settled in eastern and southeastern Europe during the 2nd and 3rd millennia B.C. Modern Slavs include Russians, Ukrainians, Poles, Czechs, Slovaks, Serbs, Croats, Slovenes, Macedonians, and Bulgars.

Song Dynasty
One of China's greatest dynasties (960–1279), whose rulers presided over a remarkable flowering of art and literature. The Song period also saw the invention of movable type for printing and gunpowder for use in weapons.

Srivijaya
Maritime empire that dominated much of the Malay–Indonesian archipelago from the 6th to the 14th centuries. Influenced by India and largely Buddhist, it also blended indigenous traditions.

stupa
Dome-shaped Buddhist monument representing the universe and usually containing relics of the Buddha or of a Buddhist saint.

Sui Dynasty
Short-lived Chinese dynasty founded by Yang Jian, who reunited China in 589 A.D. and ruled as the Emperor Wen. His successor, Yang, was overthrown in 618 by the first emperor of the Tang Dynasty.

suttee
Hindu custom whereby a widow committed suicide by burning herself on her husband's funeral pyre. It was banned in the 17th century by India's Mogul emperors and later by British colonial rulers.

Taika Reform
A series of measures announced by Emperor Kotuku in 646 that were intended to remodel Japanese society along Chinese lines, in the process transferring power from local lords to the emperor himself.

Takrur
A West African trading center in the Senegal Valley to the west of its rival, Ghana. Early converts to Islam, its merchants traded along the coastal route to Morocco and beyond.

Tamil
The language and culture of the peoples of southern India and Sri Lanka. The 7th century saw a renaissance in Tamil music, art, and poetry.

Tang Dynasty
A line of emperors inaugurated by Gaozu in 618 that presided over a time of immense power and prosperity for China, as well as a golden age of literature, art, and ideas. The dynasty ended with Ai Zong's overthrow in 907.

Tarim Basin
Now in the western Chinese province of Xinjiang, this area was bitterly fought over by China and Tibet in the 8th century, straddling as it did the vital east–west Silk Road.

Tendai sect
Form of Buddhism introduced into Japan from China in the early 9th century by Saicho. Its chief scripture was the *Lotus Sutra*. Followers of Tendai combined use of mystical Shingon rituals with meditation.

themes
Military districts of the Byzantine Empire. Each theme was governed by a general and settled by soldiers who, in return for land and tax exemptions, performed military service for the emperor.

Tiahuanaco
The capital of a civilization established on the southern shores of Lake Titicaca in the Bolivian Andes Mountains. Founded in about 500 A.D., the city reached the height of its influence in the late 1st millennium A.D.

Toltecs
The people who ruled central Mexico from the 9th to the 12th centuries A.D. Expert builders and metalworkers, their capital was at Tula, north of present-day Mexico City.

Tulunid Dynasty
Founded by Ahmed ibn Tulun, a provincial governor who in 868 broke free of the authority of the caliph who had appointed him, this dynasty maintained its independence of Baghdad until 905, ruling Syria and Egypt.

Uighurs
Warlike nomads from Central Asia, the Uighurs invaded both China and Tibet in the 8th century, and were soon pushing westward, building an empire that anticipated that of Genghis Khan.

Umayyad Dynasty
The successors of Umar, who ruled the Islamic world as caliphs after the Prophet Muhammad's death; their legitimacy long challenged, they were overthrown by the Shiite Abbasids in 750.

Vandals
A Germanic people who invaded the Roman Empire in 406–409 A.D. and settled in Spain. In 429 they reached North Africa and established a kingdom there, from which they attacked Rome in 455. The Vandal Kingdom survived until 534.

Varangians
Swedish Vikings who founded Rus and opened up trading routes to Byzantium and the Arab lands. The name may come from an Old Norse word meaning "men of the pledge," or confederates.

Vedas
Literally "books of knowledge," a series of sacred poems dating back to India's Aryan period and probably composed from about 1500 to 900 B.C. The hymns set out the ordering principles not only of Hinduism but of Aryan society in general.

Vinland
Norse name for the area of North America, probably on the Newfoundland coast, that the Viking adventurer Leif Eriksson visited in about the year 1000 A.D. It was named for the wild grapes (possibly gooseberries or cranberries, for grapes could not have grown so far north) that Leif claimed to have found there. The remains of a Viking settlement have been found at L'Anse-aux-Meadows in northern Newfoundland.

Visigoths
A Germanic people related to the Ostrogoths who invaded the Roman Empire in 376 A.D. and founded a kingdom in southwestern France and Spain.

Wei
The northernmost, as well as the richest and most populous, of the three kingdoms into which China was divided after the collapse of the Han Dynasty in 200 A.D. The other two were Shu and Wu.

Yamato kings
The rulers of the Yamato Plain on the island of Honshu who gradually extended their authority throughout the whole of Japan between the 4th and 8th centuries A.D. They were strongly influenced by Chinese culture.

Zapotecs
A people of ancient Mexico, living in the Oaxaca Valley, who developed the earliest script in the Americas. Their most important center was at Monte Albán, which flourished between 400 B.C. and 700 A.D.

Zoroastrianism
Religion founded by Zoroaster (also known as Zarathustra), a Persian prophet of the 6th century B.C., which sees the world and history in terms of a struggle between the forces of good and evil. It is still practiced by a few communities in Iran and by the Parsis of western India.

FURTHER READING

Barbero, Alessandro. *Charlemagne, Father of a Continent*. Berkeley, CA: University of California Press, 2004.

Becher, Matthias. *Charlemagne*. New Haven, CT: Yale University Press, 2003.

Berrin, Kathleen, and Esther Pasztory. *Teotihuacán: Art from the City of the Gods*. New York: Thames & Hudson, 1994.

Coe, Michael D. *The Maya*. New York, NY: Thames & Hudson, 2005.

Fash, William L. *Scribes, Warriors, and Kings: The City of Copán and the Ancient Maya*. New York, NY: Thames & Hudson, revised edn., 2001.

Friedel, David, and Linda Schele. *A Forest of Kings: The Untold Story of the Ancient Maya*. New York, NY: Quill/W. Morrow, reprint edn., 1992.

Friedel, David, Linda Schele, and Joy Parker. *Maya Cosmos: Three Thousand Years on the Shaman's Path*. New York, NY: W. Morrow, 1993.

Geary, Patrick. *Before France and Germany: The Creation and Transformation of the Merovingian World*. New York, NY: Oxford University Press, 1988.

Hall, John Whitney. *Japan: From Prehistory to Modern Times*. Ann Arbor, MI: University of Michigan Press, reprint edn., 1991.

Hempel, Rose. *The Golden Age of Japan*. New York, NY: Rizzoli, 1983.

Hodgson, Marshall G.S. *The Venture of Islam Vol.1: The Classical Age of Islam*. Chicago, IL: University of Chicago Press, reprint edn., 1977.

Humphreys, R. Stephen. *Islamic History: A Framework for Inquiry*. Princeton, NJ: Princeton University Press, revised edn., 1991.

Jones, Gwyn. *A History of the Vikings*. New York, NY: Oxford University Press, 2nd edn., 2001.

Lewis, Bernard. *The Arabs in History*. New York, NY: Oxford University Press, 6th edn., 2002.

Massie, Suzanne. *Land of the Firebird: The Beauty of Old Russia*. New York, NY: Simon and Schuster, 13th edn., 1980.

Miller, Mary, and Karl Taube. *An Illustrated Dictionary of the Gods and Symbols of Ancient Mexico and the Maya*. New York, NY: Thames & Hudson, 1997.

Miller, Mary Ellen, and Linda Schele. *The Blood of Kings: Dynasty and Ritual in Maya Art*. New York, NY: George Braziller, reprint edn.,1992.

Norwich, John Julius. *A Short History of Byzantium*. New York, NY: Knopf, reprint edn., 1998.

Pasztory, Esther. *Teotihuacán: An Experiment in Living*. Norman, OK: University of Oklahoma Press, 1997.

Pirenne, Henri. *Mohammed and Charlemagne*. Mineola, NY: Dover Publications, reprint edn., 2001.

Riasanovsky, Nicholas V. *A History of Russia*. New York, NY: Oxford University Press, 6th edn., 1999.

Rodinson, Maxime. *Muhammad*. New York, NY: New Press, 2002.

Roesdahl, Else. *The Vikings*. New York, NY: Penguin, 2nd edn., 199.

Sansom, George. *A History of Japan to 1334*. Stanford, CA: Stanford University Press, 1965.

Saunders, J.J. *A History of Medieval Islam*. New York, CA: Routledge, revised edn., 1990.

Sawyer, Peter. *The Oxford Illustrated History of the Vikings*. New York, NY: Oxford University Press, 2001.

Talbot Rice, David. *The Dawn of European Civilization: The Dark Ages*. New York, NY: McGraw-Hill, 1965.

Treadgold, Warren. *A History of the Byzantine State and Society*. Stanford, CA: Stanford University Press, 1997.

Wood, Ian. *The Merovingian Kingdoms 450–751*. New York, NY: Longman, 1994.

SET INDEX